The Forest of
BOWLAND
& PENDLE HILL

• HALSGROVE DISCOVER SERIES ➤

The Forest of
BOWLAND
& PENDLE HILL

An Area of Outstanding Natural Beauty

Andy Stansfield

HALSGROVE

First published in Great Britain in 2006

Copyright © 2006 Andy Stansfield
All photographs in this book are by Andy Stansfield except where indicated otherwise
The right of Andy Stansfield to be identified as the author of this work has been asserted
by him in accordance with the Copyright, Design and Patents Act 1988 (UK)

Frontispiece photograph: *The hen harrier, symbol of the Forest of Bowland AONB.*
Courtesy of Richard Saunders, Hen Harrier Recovery Project Manager, English Nature

Disclaimer
While the author has walked all the routes described in the book, no responsibility can be
accepted for any omissions or errors or for any future changes that may occur in the details given.
The author and publisher cannot accept any liability for accident, mishap,
or loss arising from the use of this book.

British Library Cataloguing-in-Publication Data
A CIP record for this title is available from the British Library

ISBN 1 84114 517 3
ISBN 978 1 84114 517 4

HALSGROVE
Halsgrove House
Lower Moor Way
Tiverton, Devon EX16 6SS
Tel: 01884 243242
Fax: 01884 243325
email: sales@halsgrove.com
website: www.halsgrove.com

Printed and bound by D'Auria Industrie Grafiche Spa, Italy

Contents

WALKS

Acknowledgements

The author gratefully acknowledges the support of the following:
English Nature especially Jon Hickling, Richard Saunders and Stephen Murphy
David Sowter and Simon Hawtin
Robert Bassendon of Wray village
RSPB especially Pete Wilson, Anna Sugrue, Tom Bridge and Gavin Thomas
Anne Gardner of Lower Fair Snape Farm
Andrew Turner of Malkin Tower Farm
Nigel Pilling and Louise Wylie of United Utilities
Clitheroe Information Centre (Lancs CC)
Lancashire County Council Environment Directorate especially the AONB team
Rod Banks of Abbeystead Estate

THE FOREST OF BOWLAND AONB

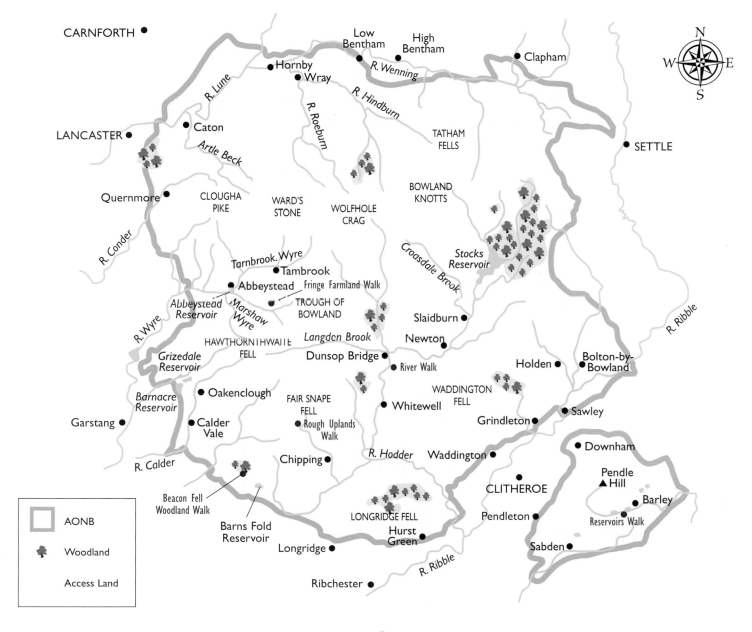

CARNFORTH

Low
Bentham
High
Bentham

Clapham

Hornby
Wray
R. Wenning

R. Lune
R. Hindburn

Caton
R. Roeburn
TATHAM
FELLS
SETTLE

LANCASTER

Artle Beck

Quernmore
CLOUGHA
PIKE
WARD'S
STONE
WOLFHOLE
CRAG
BOWLAND
KNOTTS

R. Conder

Stocks
Reservoir

Croasdale Brook

Tarnbrook. Wyre
Tambrook
Abbeystead
Fringe Farmland Walk
TROUGH OF
BOWLAND
Slaidburn
R. Ribble

Abbeystead
Reservoir
Marshaw
Wyre
Langden Brook
Newton

R. Wyre
HAWTHORNTHWAITE
FELL
Dunsop Bridge
River Walk
Holden
Bolton-by-
Bowland

Grizedale
Reservoir
WADDINGTON
FELL

Barnacre
Reservoir
Oakenclough
FAIR SNAPE
FELL
Whitewell
Grindleton
Sawley

Garstang
Calder
Vale
Rough Uplands
Walk
Downham

R. Calder
Chipping
R. Hodder
Waddington
Pendle
Hill
CLITHEROE

Beacon Fell
Woodland Walk
LONGRIDGE FELL
Pendleton
Barley

Barns Fold
Reservoir
Hurst
Green
Reservoirs Walk

Longridge
Sabden

Ribchester
R. Ribble

N
W   E
S

Legend:

- AONB
- Woodland
- Access Land

7

1. Outstanding Natural Beauty

Defining the boundaries of the area to be covered by a book such as this is always contentious in that, like a wedding invitation list, it is always likely to exclude a worthy participant. In this case, it was decided to adopt a ready-made boundary in the form of that used by the Forest of Bowland Area of Outstanding Natural Beauty (AONB).

The purpose of this book is to convey to the reader the true character of the area of greatest interest, and the AONB boundary usefully excludes some landscapes and communities which are not typical of the rough uplands and their hinterland, but which lie within the same administrative boundaries. The best example of this is the inclusion of Pendle Hill, albeit as a second distinct area, within the AONB. Pendle Hill itself demands to be considered alongside the upland areas of the Forest of Bowland but the administrative boundary of Pendle rolls in the industrial heritage towns of Lancashire to its south-east which, whilst of great interest, do not belong in this volume.

Pendle Hill from the south west.

Opposite: *The essential character of the Forest of Bowland.*

9

Similarly, the AONB boundary excludes all but a small section of the Ribble Valley, which has a quite different character, running between Pendle and The Forest of Bowland.

There are forty Areas of Outstanding Natural Beauty in England, Wales and Northern Ireland comprising 18 per cent of the land area. Each has been designated by the Countryside Agency or its predecessors for the prime purpose of conserving and enhancing natural beauty.

The Countryside Agency defines the natural beauty of AONBs as being 'partly due to nature, and partly the product of many centuries of human modification of natural features. Landscape encompasses everything, natural and human, that makes an area distinctive: geology, climate, soil, plants, animals, communities, archaeology, buildings, the people who live in it, past and present, and perceptions of those who visit it.'

River Hodder at Whitewell. © Lancs CC

Enhancing recreation and the enjoyment of that natural beauty, however, is not one of the criteria for designation. The main focus for the designating body is to protect the area while recognising the needs of the rural economy and of the communities within the chosen boundary. Every attempt is made to promote sustainable development which, in itself, conserves and improves the environment.

However AONBs differ from National Parks, despite originally being designated under the same legislation provided by the National Parks and Countryside Act (1949), in that they do not have the single body responsible for planning and development which plays such an influential role in each National Park.

The Forest of Bowland Area of Outstanding Natural Beauty was designated in 1964 and is situated in north-west England, predominantly in Lancashire except for its north-east corner which lies in Yorkshire, and covers 312 square miles with a resident population of a mere 16,000.

Pheasants are a common sight.

It was chosen because of its essential tranquillity and the great variety of its scenery: isolated upland plateaux, well-defined river valleys of varying age, escarpments and undulating lowlands, an extensive range of indigenous and migratory birds, both local and imported wildlife, together with scattered agricultural communities having

Opposite: *Salisbury Hall, Newton.*

11

Several county boundary markers have been redundant since the 1974 boundary changes.

Local people are also an important part of the landscape.

a strong sense of heritage and tradition. Its bio-diversity is of both national and international importance.

Consisting largely of a core of moorland which is fringed by farmland, it is drained by the Rivers Ribble, Hodder, Wyre and Lune. The upland core is divided into two significant land masses by the Trough of Bowland – an historic route along which several of the Pendle Witches were transported for trial in the county town of Lancaster. Pendle Hill forms a third outlying land mass. The Forest of Bowland is not a forest in the woodland sense. Rather, the term is a medieval one meaning an extensive tract of open country, often used for hunting and usually reserved for the reigning monarch.

In fact there were four Royal Forests in the area: Bowland, Wyresdale, Quernmore, and Bleasdale. The Royal Forest of Bowland covered a much smaller area than the Forest of Bowland is deemed to cover now. In addition to the Royal Forests, the northern valleys of the Hindburn and Roeburn were also used for hunting, and there were also enclosed deer parks like the one on the Leagram estate near Chipping.

Alert young rabbit.

Cow Ark Farm.

Milestone dated 1739 along the historic route through the Trough of Bowland.

TEN BEST VIEWPOINTS

Pendle Hill
Beacon Fell
Jubilee Tower
Longridge Fell & Jeffrey Hill
Bowland Knotts
Parlick Fell
Entrance to Higher Fencewood Farm
(1mile SW of Burholme Bridge)
Twiston
Mallowdale Pike
Clougha

Summit of Beacon Fell.

Jubilee Tower affords fabulous views over Morecambe Bay.

Today the Forest of Bowland is a major recreational resource for the Lancashire towns north of Manchester. The most popular resource, Beacon Fell Country Park (which includes Bowland Visitor Centre), attracts 260,000 day visitors each year. Pendle Hill provides a more focused destination than the Forest of Bowland, largely for ramblers and those wishing to tour the villages of Pendle Witch country.

As this manuscript is being prepared for publication, changes are taking place which will have further impact upon the delivery of services within AONBs and National Parks, along with other areas of significant character, whether rural or urban. The Countryside Agency's role is being split in two by new legislation as a result of DEFRA's Rural Strategy paper, published in July 2004. In March 2006, the Natural Environment and Rural Communities Act received Royal Assent and will come into force in October 2006.

Beacon Fell. © Lancs CC

Firstly, this Act will establish the completely independent Commission for Rural Communities to act as adviser, advocate and independent watchdog. This is to be created out of the present division of the Countryside Agency which currently handles these matters. Secondly it will create a single body, Natural England, which will combine the present Landscape, Access and Recreation division of the Countryside Agency plus DEFRA's Rural Delivery Service with English Nature.

The new Natural England agency will be responsible for enhancing bio-diversity, landscapes and wildlife in rural, urban and coastal areas as well as promoting public access to and recreation within those areas. Its management of all the natural and human resources involved, given the complexity of the partnership arrangements I've discovered in researching just this one area, will be an awesome task indeed.

As the original 1949 legislation governing the designation of National Parks does not clearly define 'natural beauty' there is an urgent need, legally speaking, to do so. It is more probable, at this time, that a definition will be appended to one of several other pieces of legislation but we all wait with bated breath. This development alone has the potential for significant impact, especially if further challenges are allowed retrospectively, and not just on National Parks because the same legislation for designation is also used for Areas of Outstanding Natural Beauty.

An Environment Agency employee checking water quality at Stoops Bridge, Abbeystead.

PROJECTS AND PARTNERSHIPS

The effective management of a complex, organic system such as an AONB requires from its officers nothing less than a total commitment to the prime objectives of conservation and the enhancement of natural beauty. But when those who influence the decision-making process are also representatives of a wide variety of organisations, each with a vast range of concerns of which the AONB is but one, that is no easy thing to achieve.

The AONB Joint Advisory Committee, which provides liaison between all the interested parties, is made up of representatives from no fewer than 20 different bodies. Many different local authorities are represented, along with DEFRA, English Nature, Environment Agency, and recreational bodies like the Ramblers' Association, as well as the RSPB and the Countryside Agency. United Utilities has a place at the table too, as befits one of the major landowning partners, with the Forest of Bowland Landowning and Farming Advisory Group also playing a part.

It is important to recognise that most AONB land is privately owned and agricultural in nature. As such, there are few statutory restrictions on land-use by those landowners except where Sites of Special Scientific Interest (SSSIs) are found on

The Duchy of Lancaster's Whitewell Estate is one of several large estates in the AONB.

Welcome sign with access information.

SEVEN USEFUL ACRONYMS

AONB	Area of Outstanding Natural Beauty
DEFRA	Department for Environment, Food and Rural Affairs
CRoW Act	Countryside and Rights of Way Act, 2000
PMG	Partnership Management Group
JAC	Joint Advisory Committee
RSPB	Royal Society for the Protection of Birds
SSSI	Site of Special Scientific Interest

their land. The active participation of landowners in the processes of conservation and enhancement of the AONB's natural beauty is possibly the most vital element of all. With the introduction of the Countryside and Rights of Way Act (2000), increasing access for designated recreational purposes (in some cases facilitating access for the very first time into some upland areas such as parts of the Forest of Bowland) the landowner's role has become even more crucial.

While the Joint Advisory Committee has a vital role in influencing the strategies adopted, it does not play its part in isolation. It is supported by the Partnership Management Group which represents the funding partners – essentially the local authorities and the Countryside Agency. The PMG's role is to monitor budget and policy matters such as overseeing the allocation of funds from the AONB Project Fund. Another advisory role is played by the Officers' Technical Committee, again comprised of representatives from partner organisations, which provides technical professional guidance to the JAC when making its recommendations.

Partnership isn't always about large organisations and public bodies either; the Parish Lengthsman project being a case in point. Although this project, initially launched in 1998 as a pilot scheme in the Bowland area, owes its existence to partnership between County, District and Parish Councils, the implementation of it comes down to each individual Parish Lengthsman operating within his own respective parish boundaries.

The role of Parish Lengthsman is not a new concept. Originally this person was employed to maintain pathways, roadside verges and drainage in his own parish but with the reintroduction of the role a number of environmental tasks were added,

Hen harriers are a protected species.
© R Saunders

Hen harriers are wing-tagged to monitor their movements. © D Sowter

plus the Lengthsman may work within a number of parishes in partnership. The advantage of having someone local to fulfil this role is that work can often be carried out immediately without having to compete for priority with more urgent jobs in other areas. At the time of writing the AONB has two operating Parish Lengthsmen in Dave Bridge, who is the Pendle Hill Lengthsman, and Richard Atton, who acts for Bolton by Bowland.

The Birds of Bowland Project is a partnership with a very precise focus, run by the RSPB in partnership with United Utilities with support from Lancashire Rural Futures. It was previously supported in part by the Heritage Lottery Fund which funded a community post, that person working closely with local schoolchildren. As that funding ceased, so did the work with schools. This is not untypical of the way that initiatives follow the funding, but it is frustrating that continuity cannot be maintained.

A key aspect of the Birds of Bowland Project is the work done in conjunction with English Nature on the Hen Harrier Recovery Project, which was launched by English Nature in 2002. So great was the concern for their future, wing-tagging of young hen harriers in this area began back in 1998, and the RSPB has been monitoring Bowland's breeding hen harrier population since 1981. The hen harrier is one of our rarest raptors and has been adopted as the symbol of Bowland AONB, its image being seen on every AONB roadside sign and logo.

From a promising but still vulnerable position of there being 22 nesting attempts by hen harriers in the north of England in 2003, during 2004 that number fell dramatically to 10, all of which lay within Bowland AONB. Of these 10, eight were on United Utilities land, hence the importance of their involvement. These eight nesting sites were unusually productive with 25 chicks being reared that year whereas in 2005, 11 nesting attempts produced just 19 young.

Interestingly, peregrines also had a bumper year in 2004 with 11 young being produced from seven nesting sites but, once again, these figures dropped in 2005 when six pairs reared just five young between them.

Hen harrier movements are being monitored by fitting young birds with coloured wing tags, each with an identification code so that individual birds can be monitored as well as the general trend. It should be remembered that is illegal to approach the nesting sites of protected species. If you are interested in seeing hen harriers or, indeed, other birds of prey, then the RSPB lead guided walks for this purpose. Details of these and other RSPB events are usually posted in the events section of the AONB website, or you can contact the RSPB North West England Regional Office in Huddersfield on 01484 861148 for information.

Another project United Utilities has been involved in for the past couple of years involves attempts to reintroduce the otter, which is a listed species in the United Utilities Bio-diversity Action Plan. Five otter holts have now been constructed to provide somewhere for the otters to lay up during the day and, hopefully, in which to breed. Two of these are on the shores of Stocks Reservoir and two are on the River Hodder, popular places with visitors, but their exact locations are a closely-guarded secret for obvious reasons. United Utilities Ranger Nigel Pilling and Wildlife Warden Morris Kettlewell are responsible for constructing and maintaining the holts, but it is still too early to report significant results or even to guess at the extent of the otter population.

United Utilities Ranger Nigel Pilling.

Stocks Reservoir has two otter holts.

Left: *Peter Dennis and Vicky Sweeney conducting a fish and vertebrates survey in the Hodder catchment area for APEM Ltd on behalf of United Utilities.*

Male otters are able to cover a vast area: any in the Hodder valley are quite capable of extending their territory over into the Lune valley, for example. So far, only occasional signs of usage have been found at the holts, to the extent that it is impossible to say whether these are signs of several otters or just one. Nigel Pilling confirms that there are no indications at all of any breeding taking place within the AONB area. Nevertheless, two more holts are planned for the coming year, along with the possibility of additional planting alongside sections of the Hodder to increase vegetation cover for these delightful but extremely shy animals.

The Lancashire Rural Recovery Action Plan is an initiative which was launched in 2002 by the Lancashire Rural Partnership in the wake of the Foot and Mouth outbreak and which, not least because of the impact of that dreadful epidemic, has great meaning in the AONB area. It claimed at the time to be the first such strategy and action plan to consider rural economic decline and long-term rural regeneration on a county-wide basis. Since its inception this Action Plan has succeeded in providing over £7million-worth of funding for a variety of initiatives and, in so doing, has helped to create and safeguard 400 jobs for local people in Lancashire, including the Bowland AONB.

Arising out of a project called the Bowland Initiative, Lancashire Rural Futures is an organisation now partly funded by the Rural Recovery Action Plan and its aims are essentially the same. Recognising correctly that there would be radical changes in the way subsidies were going to shift from core farming to agricultural diversification and environmental schemes, Lancashire Rural Futures offers support and advice to farmers and rural businesses with these trends in mind. Projects receiving assistance have included the regeneration of hedgerows and stone walls, tree planting, the protection of watercourses, the management of wildlife habitats, the renovation of buildings, renewable energy projects and the development of community workshops. Some specific examples are examined in a different context in later chapters.

While the profusion of agencies and organisations involved in the management of the physical, social and economic landscape is more than a little confusing, several factors become clear. There is a continuing need to identify and monitor the most vulnerable aspects of the AONB; there is now appreciable funding momentum being gained in the protection of livelihoods and buildings of rural character; and,

New opportunities for funding help to protect traditional livelihoods.

Opposite: *Stone walls are an integral feature of the landscape.*

lastly, there is a high level of awareness of the risk posed to a wide range of habitats by even the slightest change in the eco-system of the area.

Given the high profile of rural and environmental issues, one might be forgiven for assuming that the vast majority of local people would be directly affected by either the problems or their solutions, but that is not the case. One of the most surprising employment statistics is that only 11 per cent of the resident population is involved with agriculture and forestry. Compare that with the figures for manufacturing (15 per cent), real estate (10 per cent) and the combined figures for education and health or social work sectors (22 per cent) and you have a clearer overview of the actual lifestyles of the AONB's residents.

A VISION FOR THE FUTURE

When admiring the rich greens and subtle shifts of tone in the woodlands in summer; when stunned by the splendid isolation of stone barns in upland pastures, or when awestruck by the sheer variety of mosses and lichens on a stone wall, it is all too easy to fall into the trap of feeling that the habitats of the AONB are time-less. The truth is that changes have taken place and will continue to take place, in some cases to the detriment of those habitats. The trick is to manage that change and, in some cases, attempt to reverse it.

Mosses and lichens on a wall in Gisburn Forest.

Change is sometimes so slow that it goes unnoticed, especially where close observation and monitoring is absent. The fragmentation of a habitat can occur quite easily, leading to the isolation of a species and ultimately leading to its disappearance altogether. The same is true of archaeological sites, small communities and even individual buildings. This where the AONB Management Plan comes into its own, having first identified the complexity and variety of landscape features down to minute detail, and then having ascertained specific targets for conservation and, in some cases, restoration.

Taking pastures and meadows as an example, many visitors will simply see green fields. The AONB objectives, however, define these more specifically as species-rich grasslands and subdivide them even further as wader pasture, upland hay meadow, calcareous grassland, swamps and tall herb fan.

It is this attention to detail which marks the AONB's plans for monitoring, assessment, management and restoration as being of such great importance. In this way, it is not just individual habitats and landscape features which will survive but the whole eco-system with all its interdependent and interactive component parts. What's more, this applies not just to plant and animal habitats but to every aspect of life within the AONB boundary. It is a daunting task.

One such set of objectives identifies the need to 'support the maintenance and enhancement of the characteristic network of narrow country lanes, maintain walls, banks, hedgerows, trees, quality and bio-diversity of species-rich herb and grassland verge communities as well as traditional metal railings.' So even the access roads along which we drive, their verges, and the railings beside them, are under minute scrutiny to an extent which would dumbfound most visitors.

A typical country lane.

The future of the area is also of interest to those organisations devoted to our woodlands. The England Forestry Strategy wants to stop the fragmentation of our remaining ancient woodland by planting new stands of trees which will fill in the gaps between existing stands, thus creating larger individual areas of woodland which will be less vulnerable. This is especially important when linking stands of trees which have been identified on the Ancient Woodland Inventory.

But to balance this aim, it must be remembered that woodlands consist not only of trees but of ground level flora too. It is also necessary to look closely at open-space habitats of importance which would fall within those new woodlands, and also at the fringe habitats that currently exist and additional ones which will be created.

The preferred means of extending native species of broadleaved woodland is by natural regeneration or 'colonisation'. This is far easier where there are stands of trees substantial enough to produce a high volume of seeds but it is a slow, and therefore more risky, process and it is necessary to ensure that the newly seeded area is free from grazing, whether domestic or wild. Some of the types of tree best suited to such natural colonisation include hawthorn, rowan, birch and ash.

An isolated stand of silver birch with rhododendrons in a meadow in Over Wyresdale.

Planting is obviously a quicker means to an end than relying on natural colonisation but it is harder to achieve a natural-looking result and it is therefore preferable to use trees grown locally from native species. On a smaller scale, these plans will be implemented by regenerating clough woodlands, whereas the new planting of native species of trees in the valleys will have a larger visual impact in the long run.

However, English Nature also identifies several categories of land unsuitable for developing new native woodland including land above 400 metres and land with deep peat soils, either or both of which accounts for a lot of the upland area of Bowland and Pendle Hill.

As for that vision of the future, the long-term aim is that the AONB will retain that which makes it special, restore aspects of value which it has lost, and create a management framework which ensures that a set of values is incorporated into every decision-making process at all levels of activity, be it individual, social, economic, recreational or agricultural in nature. The vision, then, is not so much one which entails a different-looking landscape. It is a hidden, all-pervading way of thinking.

Opposite: Only pockets of trees remain in a landscape once completely covered by ancient woodland.

2. Physical Geography

The rocks of the Bowland area are all sedimentary in origin, having been laid down during the Carboniferous era between 345 and 280 million years ago when what is now land was covered by a shallow sea known as the Bowland Basin. The deposits, comprised of skeletal remains, underwater plants and sand and gravels which accumulated at the bottom of this sea, were compacted by pressure and later formed into folds by lateral compression.

The upland core of the Forest of Bowland, cleft in two by the Trough, consists of relatively weather-resistant sandstone known as Millstone Grit, dating from just over 300 million years ago. This tough rock cap is seen exposed at a number of places, notably Ward's Stone (560m), Bowland Knotts (428m) and Clougha Pike (413m), but it is largely covered with blanket bog and moorland grasses.

Once the sea had receded, due partly to an uplift of landmass and partly to climate change, subsequent erosion was effected by the weather and, more particularly, by the ice sheet which covered the area between roughly two million years ago and only 10,000 years ago. The tops of the folds, in most cases, were scrubbed off to reveal bands of many differently classified rocks, although all were formed during a relatively narrow time-frame (in geological terms) and are collectively referred to as the Namurian Series. The overall shape of the landscape was determined by this glaciation, and the subsequent meltwater channels which now form the principal river valleys of the Ribble, Wyre, Hodder and Lune.

The wild expanse of windblown plateau gives way to clearly defined hills around its fringes, still extensively covered by blanket bog with the added colour of heather where the peat is not waterlogged. The level of acidity in the ground is incredibly high and supports only a narrow range of grasses and reeds. These surrounding hills have been shaped more characteristically because they are of alternating bands of softer rock than the Millstone Grit, mostly shales and sandstones but still Carboniferous in origin.

Layers of sandy deposits can be seen clearly when the rock is freshly exposed.

Opposite: *Exposed gritstone at Bowland Knotts.*

Colourful mix of upland plant species.

TEN INTERESTING PLACE-NAMES

Thick Sod Holes
Castle of Cold Comfort
Apronful Hill
Salt Pie
Shivering Ginnel
Ox Pasture End
Fishes and Peggy Hill
Dead Man's Stake Clough
The Wife
Cow Ark

Trough of Bowland.

Pendle Hill is capped with Millstone Grit too, in this case a band 240-metres thick and the oldest Millstone Grit sandstone to be found in the Central Pennines. It has given its name to its own particular brand of thin-bedded fine sandstone, known as Pendle Grit. This is exposed at the two disused quarries at Nick o' Pendle, the pass which carries the road from Clitheroe over the south-western flank of Pendle Hill to Sabden.

Bentham, in particular, is well-known to geologists for its unusual set of sequences of Namurian rocks. Two examples of particular interest can be found at Eskew Beck and at Low Bentham Weir. Other classic sites include the Sykes Anticline at Rams Clough in the Trough of Bowland and Little Mearley Clough Site of Special Scientific Interest. Little Mearley Clough lies on the western slopes of Pendle Hill, above the listed buildings of Little Mearley Hall, and the stream which drains the clough has cut down through the rock strata to reveal a sequence of rock layers laid down 320 million years ago. The rock sequence exposed covers the entire duration of the oldest subdivision of the Namurian period, named the Pendleian Stage after the hill itself.

Pendle Hill. © Lancs CC

Classic glaciated landscape of Fiendsdale and Langden Brook.

Large scale maps are essential in this terrain.

LAND USE

Ordnance Survey maps at 1:25,000 scale show stone walls and enclosures which reveal something of the history of land enclosure and agricultural usage. Increased clearance of woodland areas and the growing number of farming hamlets in the valleys during the Middle Ages led to a field system which is still easily recognisable on maps today.

Each village, often no more than a tiny hamlet in fact, had a number of enclosed fields which supported its occupants. This was an extension of the feudal strip system in which each family had a number of small strips of land, not necessarily adjacent to one another. Beyond the enclosed fields surrounding each village would be areas of common grazing, also enclosed.

As the local population increased, especially from the sixteenth century onwards, attempts were made to convert additional land, previously deemed unusable, such as the fell-sides. With this expansion of agricultural land came the increased development of isolated farms as village inhabitants moved out of the closely-knit hamlets. Some of the best examples of old farming hamlets surrounded by relatively small enclosed fields with adjacent though larger enclosed pastures on the fell-sides, once common grazing land, can be found in the dead-end valleys of which there are so many in the AONB.

The single most important factor in determining land use in the area is that of soil type. On the upland fells the high rainfall, persistent wind and subsequently lower temperatures, and absence of drainage has resulted in widespread blanket bog and a peat base which may be up to ten feet (3m) deep or more in places. Such a harsh environment can be expected to be of little use other than occasional rough grazing and the development of a grouse shooting regime. Even around the moorland fringe farming is far from easy. As the AONB Management Plan points out:

The Forest of Bowland area is classified as an upland farming area; even the lower lying farms around the moorland fringe are classified as upland farms largely due to the climate and soil type even though they appear to be in a lowland situation.

Unusual carved sandstone gatepost of indeterminate age – one of many around Newton.

Tarnbrook is a classic farming hamlet. The dwelling pictured dates back to 1730.

31

Typical fringe farmland and heather moorland.

Farms in the AONB are, on average, almost twice the size of those in Lancashire as a whole: an indication of the relatively poor quality of the grazing rather than a sign of affluence among the landowners. In these fringe areas, animal husbandry is dedicated to beef cattle and sheep, the latter being also for meat production since the price of wool has reached such a low ebb. In the lower valleys and flood plains sheep are still a major feature but dairy farming also has a substantial place.

The 2002 DEFRA Agriculture Census indicated a sheep population within the AONB of 310,666 and a cattle population of 50,068, with dairy herds being roughly three times the size of beef herds. These figures showed almost identical reductions of around 20 per cent in both sheep and cattle numbers compared with the previous year: a graphic illustration of just how devastating the 2001 Foot and Mouth epidemic was, and despite the fact that some restocking may well have taken place by the time the census was taken. It's no wonder that farmers have welcomed recent initiatives to diversify following the impact of such an epidemic.

Autumn hues brighten up the broadleaved woodland in the Dunsop valley.

Three-year-old Swaledale ram.

Swaledale sheep are the most common breed in the area.

Bowland is a seemingly timeless landscape but it is continually undergoing subtle changes.

But it's not only farming practices which have been led down the path of diversification. With more and more grants and subsidies aimed at diversifying the nature of existing conifer plantations and regenerating some of the broadleaved woodland which has disappeared over the centuries, the character of Bowland's woodland is changing too. These changes are slow and small-scale but significant because of the effect they will ultimately have on both the natural and economic environments.

Plantations of conifers, established in the mid-twentieth century, are no longer simply a source of timber: the Forestry Commission now plays an active role in conservation and recreation in partnership with other organisations. There is also a well-established trend towards using locally-grown timber, from sustainable sources, for projects within the AONB such as creating gates, stiles and fingerposts.

FRAMEWORKS FOR CONSERVATION

But the Forest of Bowland AONB is not simply a large area of open countryside, neither on the fells nor in the valleys. While it may appear a tough uncompromising landscape which has remained largely unchanged for centuries, it is in fact a very sensitive one. Testament to this is the fact that almost 40,000 acres (approximately 62 square miles) of the AONB are designated as Sites of Special Scientific Interest, the single largest of these encompassing the main upland block which is also designated a Special Protection Area for birds.

All Special Protection Areas owe their existence to the EC Directive on Conservation of Wild Birds which requires member states to safeguard the habitats of both indigenous and migratory wild birds, with emphasis on any which are under threat. This European Directive has informed other legislation within the UK but still exists as European legislation in its own right. Every SPA, which applies only to birds, is automatically an SSSI or ASSI but provides a greater degree of protection than either of these.

Another form of protection which is European in origin is the Special Area of Conservation, of which there are also several in the AONB. These SACs are the result of the Directive on the Conservation of Natural Habitats and of Wild Fauna and Flora which clearly complements the EU Directive on Conservation of Wild

Wild birds like this curlew are protected by a wide range of UK and European legislation.

Tormentil's tiny yellow flowers among young heather shoots.

Shaggy ink cap.

Lady's smock is common in damp meadows.

Birds, adding increased protection for flora and fauna and their respective habitats. But protection isn't always statutory in nature. In addition to SSSIs, SPAs and SACs, there are nearly 500 identified wildlife sites within the AONB which are part of a countrywide network of non-statutory sites which are known variously as Biological Heritage Sites in Lancashire and as Sites of Importance for Nature Conservation in Yorkshire.

Nevertheless, it is the Sites of Special Scientific Interest with which most readers will be familiar, and in the Bowland AONB they cover a wide range of features. These range from pronounced geological features, like Little Mearley Clough referred to earlier, to species-rich meadow grassland such as Myttons Meadows SSSI, one mile north west of Slaidburn. This comprises three fields adjacent to Myttons Farm, which is also a well-known Craft Centre. Just east of Slaidburn is another species-rich meadowland SSSI in Langcliff Cross Meadow.

Wood sorrel is an indicator of ancient woodland.

Other types of habitat protected by SSSI designation include exposures of marine Lower Carboniferous rocks in the Hodder valley; areas of broadleaved (probably ancient) woodland in Roeburndale; upland oak and birch woodland in Calf Hill & Cragg Woods SSSI, and Artle Dale SSSI, which hosts over 160 species of moss and liverwort.

There are also half a dozen herb-rich meadow sites, one of which is Bell Sykes Meadows SSSI. The site covers six fields of enclosed herb-rich grassland, increasingly scarce both locally and nationally, and is situated close to Slaidburn. It is this proximity which makes it an ideal example of the difficulties involved in protecting a vulnerable habitat situated close to a popular visitor attraction. At its closest point, the site is a mere 100 yards from the houses at the eastern end of the village of Slaidburn, one of the most popular of the Bowland villages.

The six fields comprising the SSSI lie adjacent to the River Hodder on its eastern side, and on the north side of the road which crosses New Bridge heading north towards Gisburn Forest. Adjacent to the bridge is a public car park and across the road, on the south side of the bridge, is one of the most popular spots in the area for a picnic, especially in spring when it is rich with daffodils. Less than a minute's walk away, over the bridge and across the road, a stile invites walkers to venture onto one of two public footpaths which pass this SSSI.

It is often the case that public footpaths pre-date an SSSI by many years and its designation does not automatically close nor divert public rights of way. However, while using those rights of way, it is an offence to intentionally or recklessly destroy or damage or disturb any characteristic features, plants or animals. Use of the term 'recklessly' is a clear indication that, in the eyes of the law, ignorance is no excuse.

TEN PLANT SPECIES FOUND IN BELL SYKES MEADOWS

Meadow foxtail
Sweet vernal grass
Red fescue
Crested dog's tail
Meadowsweet
Lady's mantle
Meadow vetchling
Eyebright
Smooth hawk's beard
Yellow rattle

Opposite: *New Bridge at Slaidburn – a popular picnic spot in spring.*

3. Access and Recreation

It should be remembered that, while National Park status brings with it a requirement to foster recreation within its boundaries, there is no such requirement in an Area of Outstanding Natural Beauty. In fact, promoting recreation in an AONB could clearly be argued as being counter-productive.

Yet it is necessary for the AONB management team to acknowledge the fact that the public will always seek to visit and enjoy such an area. There is no option other than to 'go with the flow', to create a framework within which recreation can be channelled in non-destructive ways which, if at all possible, are of benefit to those who live within the AONB.

The watchwords are 'sustainable tourism'. There is every indication that they have got it right, because the AONB has just become the first protected area in England to be awarded the European Charter for Sustainable Tourism in Protected Areas. That said, Bowland AONB suffers from much the same problem as the Peak District National Park in that it lies close to large conurbations (as many as five million people in this case), and its visitors are predominantly day-visitors who spend little money within the area.

The introduction of the Countryside and Rights of Way (CRoW) Act (2000) will test the responsibility of walkers to respect the rights of those whose land they are crossing. It is something many have fought long and hard for since the days of the Mass Trespass on Kinder Scout in the Peak District in April 1932.

There are many comparisons that can be made between the uplands of Bowland and those of the Peak, not least the fact that large areas of moorland have long since provided grouse shooting for large private estates. The western fells of Bowland in particular, prior to the CRoW Act, were well-known for their access difficulties.

Farmers welcome respectful and appreciative ramblers.

Opposite: *Walkers take a brief respite for a spot of birdwatching.*

Clougha Pike lay at the centre of an area which was designated Access Land, with the landowner granting permission for walkers to use this area, marked forbiddingly by a thick purple line on the 1:25,000 OS map. But to champions of the right to roam, this was never good enough as permission is just that, and it can always be withdrawn.

To the east of Clougha Access Area, the concessionary footpath between Grit Fell and Ward's Stone followed a ten-metre wide corridor which you had to stick to... or else. None of this endeared the Duke of Westminster, whose 19,500 acre estate covers the area, to the walking fraternity. Thankfully, we've moved on now, thanks to the new access legislation which seems to be working well, due no doubt to the vast amount of preparatory discussion and forward planning which preceded it. This wasn't simply a matter of land boundaries changing status as there were practical issues to be tackled too. For example, dozens of new kissing gates were installed, in some cases replacing ladder stiles which are less user-friendly.

Lambing season is an especially sensitive time for farmers.

Corporate ownership, too, has played its part in Bowland, with significant rainfall catchment areas being owned by water companies. Neither of these two facts of land ownership have changed but what has altered is the new climate of social inclusion which pervaded. Signage at access points, rather than commanding a list of 'thou shalt nots', is now presaged by the word 'welcome' writ in large capital letters.

The implementation of the CRoW Act was designed to be staggered across England in eight designated regions. In Bowland's case the significant date for implementation was 19 September 2004 and the newly-designated access land is now included on the recently revised Ordnance Survey Explorer Map OL41, a double-sided 1:25,000 map which covers all but the southern tips of both Bowland and Pendle areas of the AONB.

It should be noted that the CRoW Act does allow farmers and landowners the discretion to suspend or restrict access for 28 days each year, for any reason. In addition, they may apply for long-term restrictions or closures in the interests of land management, safety or fire prevention. Details of any closures or restrictions should be indicated by signs.

Opposite: Access information near Grizedale Bridge indicates dog restrictions and safety advice.

One example of such restrictions places a requirement on dog owners to keep their dog on a lead of no longer than two metres between 1 March and 31 July (the

Hen harriers are ground-nesting birds.
© D Sowter

breeding season for ground-nesting birds) and all year when near livestock. In some areas of grouse moor, dogs may be excluded entirely.

TRANSPORT LINKS

The accessibility of the Forest of Bowland AONB is also, paradoxically, its downfall in terms of visitor numbers. The M6 motorway lies within minutes of its western boundary, but much of the M6 traffic is carrying the recreational public northwards to the Lake District, only a short drive further on. Similarly, the A59 Preston to Skipton road carries people all too easily past Clitheroe, the obvious gateway to the heart of the AONB, and on to the Yorkshire Dales National Park. In addition, running parallel to this last route and to its south, the M65 now links Preston, Blackburn, Accrington, Burnley, Nelson and Colne with only a short drive to Skipton and the Yorkshire Dales at its eastern end.

It is probably true to say that most visitors to Bowland are regular aficionados who have formed a close affinity with its treasures, forsaking to a large extent those on offer in its two National Park neighbours. Certainly, over a quarter of a million day visitors frequent the Beacon Fell Country Park each year, and Gisburn Forest and Pendle Hill itself are two more of the most popular attractions.

Beacon Fell is popular all year round, but especially for sledging in winter, after a fall of snow.

A gentle walk in the Lune valley.

Southern edge of Gisburn Forest.

The vast majority of visitors to the rest of the area tend to fall into two groups: those whose primary aim is a walk or cycle ride of moderate length lasting several hours, and those whose day is based on a drive through beautiful countryside, punctuated by a relatively short walk, picnic, or a spot of bird-watching or similar activity.

For those who prefer to use public transport, a great deal of effort has been made to improve provision within the area, though these efforts have tended to focus very much on Clitheroe as the entry point to the AONB. Access by public transport to the northern dales is still poor (and non-existent to those which are cul-de-sacs), and there is still a surprising lack of options from Lancaster to the western parts of the AONB.

A useful option for bus users is the Ribble Valley Day Ranger ticket (available from bus drivers of participating services) which costs only £4 at the time of writing and which can be used on most of the local bus services in the Ribble Valley Borough area. Once again, this favours the southern parts of the AONB like Slaidburn and Chipping.

The Bowland Transit project was set up to reduce car dependency among the local population as well as to provide a service for recreational users. Its timetable is designed to fit in with local rail services to Clitheroe and the Dales Rail service to Settle. This service operates between Clitheroe and Settle, calling at Whitewell, Dunsop Bridge, Newton and Slaidburn among others along its way. Operating as the B10, it runs from Monday to Saturday during the winter and also on Sundays in summer. The summer service also operates additional buses earlier and later in the day. On Thursdays only there is an extra service from Clitheroe to Garstang via Chipping. Bowland Transit is heavily dependent upon funding which, at the time of writing, is in place until 2008.

Ramblers often start their walks from Newton Bridge, easily accessed by bus from Clitheroe

A pleasant drive over Catlow Fell.

Bus provision in the western part of the AONB has recently received a boost with the introduction of the Garstang Super 8 service which links with Stagecoach bus services from Lancaster, Preston, Blackpool and Morecambe going via Garstang, which is just north of Preston. The Super 8 makes use of 'demand responsive' extensions to its routes: if tickets are pre-booked then it will continue beyond Dolphinholme to Abbeystead or beyond Calder Vale to Oakenclough. In fact, it will make other deviations from its route if feasible and if pre-booked. Coupled with early morning and evening 'on demand' services and the fact that the bus also has a cycle rack capable of carrying two bikes, this is a small but important step towards providing the kind of improved rural service which bus companies have traditionally shunned.

WALKING

The sheer variety of walking opportunities in the AONB means that there is something to appeal to everyone, from families with toddlers to pensioners. For anyone intending to stray further than an hour from their car on unwaymarked footpaths, an OS 1:25,000 Series (2½ inches to 1 mile) map is indispensable as it includes far more detail than its 1:50,000 counterpart and field boundaries in particular. The ability to identify isolated farm buildings and the pattern of stone walls can be especially useful when the weather comes down suddenly, as it can do so effectively in the fells hereabouts.

Adequate clothing plus some sustenance should also be considered essential, along with a whistle for attracting attention in case of injury. That said, there are also plenty of places where one can walk in the wildest of scenery in complete safety.

Opposite: *Picnic in an ancient woodland setting by Marshaw Wyre.*

Lowland footpaths abound: this one runs between Dunsop Bridge and Chipping.

Glorious days like this are infrequent on the fells.

49

Children can be encouraged to study even the most common birds, like this nesting moorhen.

Wyre Way signpost.

Village stocks at Bolton by Bowland.

There have been, during the past two or three years, many guided walks organised by Lancashire Countryside Service and the Ramblers' Association which have been designed, in terms of distance and duration, to fit in with bus services in the area. However, as services are in the habit of changing due to different demands or changes in funding, it isn't wise to include examples here. Readers are advised to contact one of the County Information Offices for up to date details on what's on offer.

For walks with children, nature trails like the one in Brock valley are especially useful as they provide lots of information which can be revisited at home afterwards through activities like drawing and painting. They are excellent for encouraging children to be observant and to teach them the basics of how to behave in a countryside setting. Undoubtedly the most popular visitor attraction for children is Bowland Wild Boar Park, which has a wide variety of animals for children to observe, feed and even handle.

Those wanting more of a challenge can opt for the 45-mile Pendle Way which, though it includes considerable sections outside the AONB, combines some of the best aspects of Pendle Hill with historic Pendle Witch country. Each of its eight sections is described in detail in a series of colourful and informative leaflets complete with maps.

Another route to consider for walkers favouring a longer distance is the 28-mile North Lancashire Bridleway which is discussed in more detail in the following section on cycling and horse-riding. My own particular favourite is the Wyre Way, which includes the river's two feeders in the form of Marshaw Wyre and Tarnbrook Wyre. Sections of this route are included in the Fringe Farmland Walk in a later chapter.

Alternatively, there is the attractively named 46-mile Journey Through the Centre of the Kingdom, starting and ending at Clitheroe. The bulk of this route lies within the AONB and the places along the way will be familiar names by now. From Clitheroe the route takes in Chatburn then swings away to Bolton by Bowland, followed by Slaidburn, Dunsop Bridge, Whitewell, Chipping and Bashall Eaves before returning to Clitheroe. Leaflets covering the walk in eight sections are available in an attractive folder.

Children, like the author's daughter, Grace, love opportunities to come into contact with animals.

Right top and bottom: *Bowland Wild Boar Park.*

What is the 'Centre of the Kingdom' connection? Dunsop Bridge has been identified as the village closest to the geographical centre of the UK, and to mark the installation of its 100,000th phone box in 1992, BT placed a commemorative one in the centre of Dunsop Bridge. The tale should end there, but it doesn't.

Arguments still rage over the precise location of the centre of the UK, with many arguing that the phone box is not in the right place at all. Using the methods of calculation preferred by Ordnance Survey, the precise location is SD642565 (or SD 64188.30 56541.43 or 54°0'13.176"N 2°32'52.278"W if you want to be fussy!) which places the centre fractionally north-west of Whitendale Hanging Stones, just over 4 miles north of Dunsop Bridge. In fact, the spot is on remote boggy moorland belonging to Brennand Farm and not exactly the sort of location where a phone box would get much use.

While the Ordnance Survey did take into account the surprisingly high number of islands constituting Great Britain, 401 in total, there are alternative ways of making the calculation. If you exclude the islands, then the centre of mainland UK is a few miles away near Whalley, but if you use the centre of a rectangle covering Great Britain then the centre is much further south in Shropshire.

The Queen visiting the centre of her realm at Dunsop Bridge. She later had lunch at the Inn at Whitewell.

Dunsop Bridge Post Office and tea rooms – affectionately called Puddleducks.

Opposite: *Walking in open countryside necessitates a few precautions.*

Walking on United Utilities water catchment land.

Moody light on Pendle's southern slopes.

Downham Camping Barn can be booked through the Youth Hostels Association.

With United Utlities being a major landowner within the AONB it's no surprise that there's a good selection of walks on their land. What will be a surprise to many who have long memories of difficulties gaining access to water catchment areas is the number of leaflets detailing walks on United Utilities property. Each leaflet provides route information supported by a detailed map but also contains much useful information on reservoirs, forestry and farming, natural history and recreation according to the walk. Of all the walk leaflets available for this area, these are among the best for being concise, informative and easy to use.

Another favourite source of walking routes is a website: www.fellscape.co.uk. Simple but sufficiently informative directions are accompanied by hand-drawn maps (ie. not Ordnance Survey extracts) and my only criticisms are that A4 printouts and the relatively small text size make these slightly less easy to use in the field. The selection of walks, though, is excellent and the site is highly recommended.

September 2006 marked the third annual Pendle Walking Festival which is organised by the Regeneration Unit of Pendle Borough Council and therefore its selection of walks covers the whole borough and not just Pendle Hill. Its walk leaders are invariably people with specialised local knowledge from bodies like United Utilities and Lancashire Countryside Service. In 2005, several walks took place on and around Pendle Hill and explored not just the hill itself but some of the reservoirs and, of course, places associated with the Witches. It is hoped that Pendle Walking Festival will continue to feature on the calendar in the years to come.

With a small number of camp sites in the area combined with the Youth Hostel at Slaidburn (a converted seventeenth-century inn which is also a Listed Building) and Camping Barns at Chipping and Downham, it is possible to backpack within the AONB. But it should be remembered that the recent CRoW legislation does not permit wild camping in England and Wales in the same way that it has now become permissible in Scotland. Other activities which may interest the fittest of readers include regular fell-running and orienteering events.

There is also the annual Bowland Challenge team event (during Bowland Festival) which is a challenge-walk for teams of four to six adults which tests not just fitness but navigational skills and requires an overnight camp too. All proceeds from this popular event go towards the Bowland Pennine Mountain Rescue Team.

CYCLING AND HORSE-RIDING

Horse-riding and cycling share an important facility: both are permitted on bridle-ways. The distinction between bridleways and footpaths, both of which can be used by pedestrians of course, has achieved even greater importance with the introduction of the CRoW Act, because increased access to open countryside and common land has only been created for the benefit of walkers. Neither horse riders nor off-road cyclists have gained anything whatsoever from this otherwise welcome legislation.

Progress has been made, however, in the creation of the North Lancashire Bridleway which will, when completed, provide a circular bridleway route running through some of the best of the AONB together with adjacent coastal scenery. Several miles of new concessionary bridleway have been linked with existing stretches and the first phase is now accessible, thanks to the combined efforts of Lancashire Countryside Service, North Lancashire Bridleways Society and Lancashire Rural Futures. Starting from Denny Beck just east of Junction 34 on the M6, the first phase stretches nearly 30 miles in a south-easterly direction almost to Slaidburn before heading south-west to Chipping.

TEN WAYS TO STAY SAFE ON THE FELLS

- Obtain a regional weather forecast
- Leave a copy of your route with someone responsible
- Always carry a windproof and water-proof jacket
- Dress in layers avoiding heavy cottons (eg. jeans)
- Wear walking boots (and consider gaiters as the tops can be extremely wet)
- Carry a torch/whistle for emergencies (repeat pattern of six blasts/flashes per minute then a minute's rest)
- Carry emergency food and fluids as well as lunch (both carbohydrates and high energy foods)
- Carry a highly visible piece of clothing, material or bivvy bag
- Know how to use a 1:25,000 map and compass
- NEVER rely on a mobile phone for summoning help (service is poor at best on the fells)

Stabling facilities are on the increase in the AONB.

This project is about much more than providing a recreational route for horse riders and cyclists: it is an excellent example of the development of sustainable tourism. The new gates and waymarker posts along the route have been created from locally-harvested hardwoods by local craftsmen. Consideration has also been given to accommodation en route and a number of working farms provide bed and breakfast together with stabling for horses, as well as giving visitors an insight into sustainable farming methods.

There is also a camping barn at Chipping and a privately-owned bunkhouse (bookable through Middle Wood ecology centre) which is a mile off route in Roeburndale, one and a half miles north of High Salter Farm which is where the track known as Hornby Road meets the dead-end road that runs south from Wray along the west side of the Roeburn valley.

The Hornby Road, also known as the Salter Road, is a classic ride in itself and runs from Roeburndale virtually to Slaidburn but it is a linear route which requires transport options to be explored if tackling it in a single day. Along its length there are sections which were once trodden by Roman soldiers and it crosses some of the wildest, bleakest countryside in the UK. But if it is a sense of solitude that is sought, then this should appeal.

For shorter and less demanding rides, especially with children, Gisburn Forest is ideal. While the Forest provides three car parks, cyclists are advised to start from Cocklet Hill car park at the Forest's southern tip. There are three waymarked routes of 5.6 miles, 7.8 miles and 9.8 miles which pass through mixed coniferous and broadleaved woodland. The longest route, best done in an anti-clockwise direction, makes use of a rather more challenging extension to the 7.8 mile circuit, taking in the highest part of Gisburn Forest near Whelp Stone Crag before a rapid descent to Dob Dale Beck, the fording of which can only be described as 'interesting' when the beck is in spate.

While Gisburn Forest is extensively criss-crossed by forestry tracks and is also quite well served by public footpaths, there are no official bridleways. Cyclists are thus required to keep to the designated mountain bike routes and although horses are not catered for specifically, they are permitted to make use of any of the forest roads. Incidentally, cycle hire facilities are available at Higher High Field Farm (Bowland

Off-road fun in Gisburn Forest.

Cycle Hire 01200-446670), which lies between Slaidburn and Gisburn Forest, and delivery to a specific location may be possible by prior arrangement.

Another popular starting point for off-road cyclists uses the car park at Dunsop Bridge. The River Dunsop can be followed northwards from the village along the United Utilities service road, passing between the wooded sides of Staple Oak Fell and Beatrix Fell. When you reach the foot of Middle Knoll, the river becomes the Whitendale which forks to the right, and the Brennand which forks to the left.

Follow the latter to Brennand Farm which, together with Lower Brennand Farm close by, nestles in the bottom of this small hidden valley with its swathe of bright green pasture set amidst the russet tones of the fells which rise sharply above it. From Brennand Farm a bridleway climbs over the back of Middle Knoll, dropping into Whitendale before climbing again over the access land of Dunsop Fell then descending to meet the North Lancashire Bridleway to the north west of Slaidburn. Off-road cyclists will find this difficult going as it crosses ground on the tops which is rarely anything but saturated.

Gisburn Forest has three marked off-road cycle routes.

River Dunsop and Beatrix Fell.

Bridleway and entrance to Higher Fencewood Farm.

There is also a bridleway from Brennand Farm which follows a steep climb south-west up the Ouster Rake path onto Whin Fell. Quite how this path came to be designated a bridleway is a mystery, as the upper part of the climb up Ouster Rake is almost vertical and exceedingly treacherous in the wet. It is not passable on horseback and only the fittest off-road cyclists (with good life insurance policies to boot) would consider carrying their bike up this 400-ft/122m section. However, once on top the views are excellent though brief as the bridleway turns sharply westwards before dropping down to meet the Trough of Bowland road at Trough Barn. From here it is a short distance by road back to Dunsop Bridge.

By turning off the Dunsop Bridge–Trough road at Hareden it is possible to follow a high-level bridleway, especially popular with horse riders, which heads southwards to a point level with Whitewell, where it rejoins the road network at the entrance to Higher Fencewood Farm a mile south-west of Burholme Bridge. (The bridleway from Hareden to this point is also part of the North Lancashire Bridleway referred to earlier.)

Opposite: *Langden Brook near Hareden.*

A 'Quiet Lane' between Worston and Downham.

From here it is a downhill ride to the bridge followed by a short stretch of road alongside the River Hodder back to the village car park at Dunsop Bridge. Parking can be had either in Dunsop Bridge or at the roadside at Hareden which is a popular parking spot but perhaps less secure.

Routes like these taking in both moorland and valley bottom together with mixed woodlands make it possible to see virtually every type of habitat that Bowland has to offer, condensing the Forest of Bowland experience into a few hours, the memories of which could last a lifetime if the weather is kind and rare birds are on the wing.

QUIET LANES

One welcome initiative which is of value to both horse-riders and cyclists is the Quiet Lanes scheme, set up by the Countryside Agency and piloted by Lancashire County Council within the Bowland AONB. Roads which are designated Quiet Lanes are minor roads in rural areas which have signs to indicate their status so as to encourage greater usage by walkers, cyclists and horse-riders without actually restricting motor traffic other than to recommend proceeding with greater caution and courtesy.

In some cases, Quiet Lanes will deliberately link up with other categories of rights of way, one such example being the use of designated Quiet Lanes as part of the mostly off-road North Lancashire Bridleway.

Lancashire County Council also produce an excellent free leaflet entitled Bowland By Bike which provides details of numerous suggested routes, mostly by road and varying in length and difficulty, taking in some of the finest scenery and most interesting places in the AONB area. The most high-profile road cycling route is the Lancashire Cycleway which, though much of its 260 miles is outside the AONB, skirts the south-western boundary and does include a lengthy stretch between Waddington and Hornby, traversing some beautiful countryside en route.

OTHER RECREATIONAL OPPORTUNITIES

If you're a bird watcher then the RSPB organised walks will definitely appeal. These guided walks cover different habitats such as moorland, reservoirs and farm-

RSPB bird of prey identification walk.

land. Subject matter for the walks typically includes a hen harrier walk, wader safari, bird of prey identification walk, migratory birds, and even a walk which shows how radio tracking is used to monitor movement of certain species. Best of the lot, perhaps, is the Skydancer Safari on which, if you're fortunate, you may see the spectacular sky-dancing display of the male hen harrier.

There is a small charge for each of these walks to cover costs and all require advance booking to avoid disappointment on the day. Events are detailed on the AONB website www.forestofbowland.com/visiting/events together with a contact number for pre-booking. Some routes involve steep and awkward terrain so make enquiries beforehand with the RSPB NW England Regional Office on 01484-861148. Proper waterproofs, suitable footwear and a packed lunch are essential for all walks.

During the annual Bowland Festival in June additional guided walks include dawn chorus walks, night bat and moth walks, and local heritage trails. For the fittest of the fit, fell running and orienteering events are also staged during the course of the year by local clubs.

The RSPB's Gavin Thomas leading a Wader Safari walk.

Pendle Ski Club's dry ski slope, by the Wellsprings pub/restaurant just below Nick o' Pendle, is undoubtedly one of the greatest recreational success stories in this area. It celebrated its fortieth anniversary in 2006, and is run by a team of volunteers between October and April each year. The club itself now has 1100 members, including a couple who ski for Great Britain.

Gliding over Bleasdale.

TEN SUMMER MIGRANT BIRDS

Chiffchaff
Dotterel
Fieldfare
Garden warbler
Pied flycatcher
Redstart
Tree pipit
Wheatear
Whinchat
Whitethroat

TEN WINTER MIGRANT BIRDS

Black redstart
Black-throated diver
Brambling
Dunlin
Dunnock
Goldeneye
Pintail
Pochard
Redwing
Snow bunting

Recreation in the AONB is not confined to terra firma. Bowland Forest Gliding Club is a popular and active group operating from Lower Cock Hill Farm, beneath the distinctive 432m summit of Parlick and west of Chipping, from which there is flying on Wednesdays, Fridays and weekends when weather permits. Originally formed as The Blackpool and Fylde Gliding Club in 1950, the club operated from Blackpool Airport for fifteen years before moving to Samlesbury temporarily. Its present site was purchased in 1971 and eventually the club changed its name to reflect its new location.

Hang gliding and parascending also have their devotees in the area, with both Parlick and the fell top above Nick o' Pendle being very popular launch points.

BOWLAND FESTIVAL

One week in June every year, the Bowland Festival brings together conservation agencies, local businesses, craftsmen and artisans, and large numbers of the public in a feast of events scattered across the whole AONB. The purpose of the Festival is to 'celebrate the birds, wildlife, landscape, heritage and rural life' of the area, and it sums up the themes of this book in a host of activities spread over a nine-day period. Most importantly, it is designed to make the AONB accessible to the widest possible cross-section of the public, not just hardy bird-watchers and moorland walkers with stout boots and serious levels of fitness and stamina.

Thirty-one separate venues hosted events in the 2006 Festival, many of them repeating their programme or a variation of it several times. Coinciding with over 80 Bowland Festival events within the AONB, Clitheroe holds its own Great Days Festival during the same week. (While Clitheroe lies outside the AONB boundary, it is rightfully recognised as both a major source of visitor information and an important transport hub for those coming into the area.)

The Bowland Festival events are colour-coded in the events programme and fall within one of four themes: partnership, heritage, wildlife, and local economy. There is a predominance of wildlife and bird-watching walks, not surprisingly considering the level of RSPB involvement, but there are also walks led by Lancashire County Council's archaeologist, opportunities to learn fly fishing, and visits to the Bowland Brewery.

You can visit the eco-community and study centre of Middle Wood which is located in Roeburndale where you can camp in the woods with prior permission and there is also a bunkhouse which can be booked for groups. Craft experiences include ceramics, wood carving and a drystone walling competition. Bowland Pennine Mountain Rescue Team provide several opportunities to watch how their search and rescue dogs work, though visitors are advised that last minute cancellations are possible if the MRT is called out on an emergency – a reminder that this beautiful landscape can also be treacherous and isolated.

A wild flower recognition walk in Gisburn Forest is just one of many walking events organised for the Bowland Festival.

Cobble Hey Farm and Gardens was one of 31 venues hosting the 2006 Bowland Festival.

4. The Historic Landscape

One of the most intriguing studies to have been carried out on the AONB is the classification of the landscape by a process known as Historic Landscape Characterisation. Features are categorised into several broad groups, specifically Rough Land, Enclosed Land, Woodland, Settlement, Recreation, Ornamental, Industry, and Water. Some of these categories are then further sub-divided creating a total of sixteen identifiable landscape characters.

The combined figures for Rough Land and Enclosed Land total 92 per cent, with Woodland accounting for just over six per cent. It follows that all the remaining categories and their sub-divisions are in the fractions of one per cent. Even water, rather surprisingly, accounts for only half of one per cent.

Perhaps the most historically revealing statistics are those for the different subdivisions of Enclosed Land: only 1.62 per cent of the AONB has been enclosed since 1850. Enclosures deemed to be post-medieval (1600-1850) account for 33.8 per cent but ancient enclosures, dating back to before 1600, still account for an impressive 19.3 per cent of the AONB area. This significance is more apparent if you take the moorland out of the equation because it means that a fraction over 30 per cent of all that you see apart from the rough uplands was enclosed, farmed in some capacity, and part of a structured community before all but a handful of surviving properties were built.

At the time that all this farming landscape was evolving, the vast majority of villagers and farmers were living in timber constructions that were gradually replaced by stone-built properties between the sixteeenth and eighteenth centuries. Of these, many remain today and are most easily identified by dated inscriptions or, where a date is absent, by the characteristic stone mullions of the windows and the lintels above them. Existing buildings built prior to this, whether still complete or in ruins, tend to be ecclesiastical in origin, fortifications and fortified farms, or manor houses of which many are now farms.

Characteristic architectural features at Halton Green.

Opposite: *Old Well Hall, Downham.*

The ruins of Sawley Abbey lie just inside the AONB boundary.

A typical farming hamlet with buildings dating back to the early eighteenth century.

Date stone on a cottage in Pendleton.

Ascribing dates to periods in history is an arbitrary affair. The year 1450 is a popular choice for the end of the medieval period but 1600 is a useful starting point in a rural area for the changes that were to follow.

Forest Law had been revoked in 1507 and people were recovering from the restrictions it had placed on them. They had been prevented from extending cultivated land, planting hedges or building stone walls which might impinge on the openness and hunting quality of the four Royal Forests of Bowland, Wyresdale, Bleasdale and Quernmore. By 1600, more and more dispersed farms were springing up and this was followed by the most extensive period of enclosure with almost 62 per cent of all enclosed land being established between 1600 and 1850. The same period witnessed the building of most of the older stone properties you see in the villages today.

Bleasdale was once a hunting reserve for royalty.

Chipping Post Office. © Lancs CC

The village shop in Chipping, now also a Post Office, is claimed by some to be the oldest shop in continual usage in the country, having been built together with the adjoining house in 1668 by cloth merchant John Brabin. Since that time the shop has served the village in many forms, having been variously a grocers, a butchers, a bakers and... no, not a candlestick makers... an undertakers: the last mentioned perhaps being the most fitting, as Brabin is reputed to still haunt his house next door!

But the shop is far from being his only contribution to village life. The school on Windy Street was also the legacy of this local benefactor, together with the adjacent row of cottages which were constructed as almshouses. Both were built in the year following his death in 1683, before which he left plans to create a trust fund to provide support for the elderly poor and education for the village's children. Above the imposing doorway to the old school house is the inscription: 'This schoole founded by John Brabbin Gentleman doce disce vel discede.'

But small settlements disappear as easily as they are established, especially in an unforgiving landscape like the fells of northern England and if disease or disaster strikes either the inhabitants or their stock. Hawthornthwaite is a name which lives on through Hawthornthwaite Fell Top and the clough, Hawthornthwaite Greave, which runs off its north-west flank. But there was also a hamlet of this name once, in the Wyre valley below Hawthornthwaite Fell and midway between Cam Brow and what is now Abbeystead Reservoir. Until its demise a century ago, there was a cluster of cottages which housed workers in the bobbin mill nearby, but the mill was destroyed by fire and the cottages deserted.

Today the site of this settlement is still marked on Ordnance Survey maps but the only habitation left is a farm. Interestingly, Bob Haythornthwaite – founder of the Pennsylvania (USA) based Haythornthwaite Foundation which supports scientific research – expresses some thoughts on the evolution of his surname within this part of Bowland:

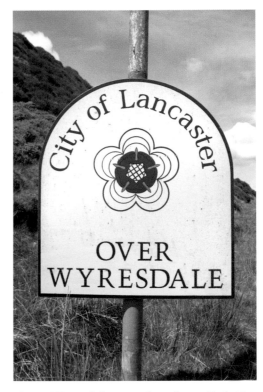

Over Wyresdale stretches from Dolphin-holme to the summit of the Trough.

The surname Haythornthwaite derives from a place-name in Over Wyresdale....It was attached officially to individuals in the sixteenth century after Henry VIII ordered parish churches to register births and deaths....and those who went north into the valley of the River Lune to villages such as Caton and Bentham came to be called Haythornthwaite, while those going south became Hawthornthwaite....

The place-name ending –*thwaite* is Norse in origin and refers to a clearing so, in this case, Hawthornthwaite referred, one assumes, to a clearing in a hawthorn thicket. While this suffix is in widespread use in the Lake District, it occurs less frequently within this area, even on the western fringes of the AONB. However, the names 'dale' and 'fell', both Scandinavian in origin, occur widely throughout, as do isolated instances of a variety of words derived from Old Norse.

EARLY SETTLEMENTS AND ROMAN ROADS

If we consider that the AONB's population today is only around the sixteen thousand mark, most of which is around the periphery, it is hardly surprising that traces of early settlement and activity are rare. Mesolithic flints have been found sporadically plus a stone axe-head at Quernmore and a Neolithic flint arrowhead on Pendle Hill. Known Bronze Age sites are few and far between with the Bleasdale

Opposite: *School and almshouses in Chipping, both built in 1684.*

69

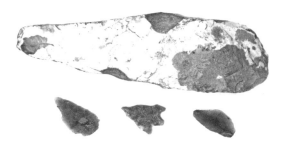

Neolithic flint arrowheads have been found on Pendle Hill.

Worked flints like this axe-head and these arrowheads have been found within the AONB.

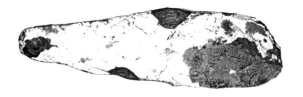

A mesolithic axe-head like this was found at Quernmore.

Timber Circle, dating back to approximately 1700 BC, being perhaps the best recorded example.

What makes this site unique is that, while timber circles and ornate burial mounds are to be found elsewhere, no other location has the two in combination.

This one consisted of two concentric circles of timber posts, with the outer circle being nearly 50 metres in diameter. The inner circle was half that size with 11 oak posts. Within the inner circle were found two decorative urns, which proved to contain cremated human bones. One of the urns also contained a small cup which probably contained sustenance for the afterlife. These are now on display in the Harris Museum in Preston. The site is located in a small copse about 600 metres north east of Bleasdale church, and can be accessed via a concessionary footpath. (Incidentally, the church is dedicated to St Eadmer, the only church in the country to be dedicated to this particular saint.)

Bronze Age artefacts have also been recovered from Whitewell, on Waddington Fell and at Pendleton, where a Bronze Age axe head was found and is now displayed at the Castle Museum in Clitheroe. The absence of Bronze Age settlements seems strange when one considers the vast quantity on Dartmoor, for example, which shares much of Bowland's upland character and can be equally inhospitable when it comes to the weather.

Following the Neolithic and Bronze Ages, with their periods of extensive tree clearance, there is little to mark the passage of time, save for some evidence of cereal farming during the Iron Age, until the arrival of the Romans. Even their legacy, at least within the AONB boundary, is largely limited to stretches of Roman road that are easier to identify on the map than in the field.

Of course, Ribchester, just outside the AONB boundary, is a famous Roman site, and features a small museum dedicated to the artefacts unearthed there, some of which have been dredged up from the waters of the Ribble itself. It plays its part here, though, because the roads which once traversed the area we are concerned with connected Ribchester with Roman sites further afield, notably Lancaster and Burrow just south of Kirkby Lonsdale.

The exact routes taken by these roads are known in part, but there are still sections where their route is easier to extrapolate from the map than from features in the landscape. With the subject having already been studied as intensively as is possible, the only new information these days tends to come from accidental discoveries made during the course of excavations for roadworks or building foundations.

It was just such a discovery, as recently as November 2005, which revealed a section of Roman road and a huge memorial stone just south of Lancaster. However, with little prospect of major roadworks taking place within the AONB, further similar discoveries are extremely unlikely.

Probably the easiest section of Roman road to identify both from the map and in the field is that crossing Jeffrey Hill, at the western end of Longridge Fell, because of the extensive views available of its route north-eastwards.

From Jeffrey Hill the route heads straight for Browsholme Heights, now a wooded hilltop, at which point it swings several degrees northwards crossing the slopes of Birkett Fell (see the River Walk: Hodder valley and Birkett Brook). It continues, straight as a die, to Croasdale, about 1½ miles west of the southern end of Stocks Reservoir.

At this point, the Roman engineers chose to swing north-westwards and for a while the route shares that of the Hornby Road track which leads over Salter Fell. This stretch, just over 3 miles in length, follows the contours of the landscape rather than adopting the straight lines one normally associates with Roman roads, before turning north to drop into the upper reaches of the Hindburn valley, continuing northwards to exit the AONB to the west of Low Bentham on its way to the fort at Burrow.

Bleasdale church.

A second suggested Roman road in the area is less well documented and may have run from Ribchester to Lancaster, bypassing Beacon Fell and making its way via Oakenclough to Street and then to Galgate where it would have joined the pre-existing north-south route to Lancaster. This route has been subject to much speculation and there is little evidence to support its existence, let alone its precise route.

A third route within the AONB proposes a road from Lancaster to Burrow along the Lune valley, supported by the finding in 1803 of a Roman milestone at a point where

Above: *Roman road half way between Jeffrey Hill and Browsholme Heights.*

Above right: *Grizedale Bridge (there are two with the same name), above Grizedale and Grizedale Lea reservoirs, may be on the route of a Roman road to Galgate.*

Right: *Swanside Bridge near Downham.*

the suggested road-line crosses Artle Beck near Caton, but once again there is more speculation than evidence. What is certain, however, is that Roman pottery and tile kilns existed at Quernmore on the western fringe of the AONB and level with Lancaster. These would certainly have required a road link with Lancaster at least.

Other evidence of early roads can be assumed from the number of ancient bridges which still remain. In some cases, for example Cromwell's Bridge near Hurst Green, new bridges have been built alongside the old bridge in order to maintain an existing route. In other examples like Swanside Bridge near Downham, a packhorse bridge in poor state of repair is the only clue to a previously existing road.

CWEORNAMOR

The Quernmore area is worthy of detailed examination because, in a relatively small area, it encompasses examples of many of the historical developments which have occurred across the whole AONB area. The name Quernmore is derived from two elements: a 'quern' is a small hand-operated mill for grinding corn and the '–more' suffix relates simply to the moor itself. The *Concise Oxford English Dictionary* identifies the roots of quern as being not just the Old Saxon 'quern' but also Old English 'cweorn', Old High German 'quirn' and Old Norse 'kvern'.

Quernmore Brow: could this be the route of a Roman road?

The inclusion of Caton and Claughton within the AONB (and by default the hilly pastoral countryside on the north side of the Lune) seems odd. In fact, with regard to historical character in particular as opposed to land use, the choice of line taken by the AONB boundary in a number of places is sometimes hard to fathom.

For example, below the western scarp of Pendle Hill the delightful and certainly one of the most typical historic villages, Pendleton, is outside the boundary, yet across the Ribble the considerably less quaint modern village of Grindleton is included. Near Lancaster, the village of Halton is excluded despite its historic links with Quernmore. Halton is the site of an eleventh century motte and bailey castle and the home of Halton Cross, believed to have been erected and carved by Norsemen 1000 years ago. A Carolingian silver cup from the late eighth or early ninth century and a Viking silver neck-ring and 860 silver coins from the era of King Cnut, all housed in the British Museum, have also been discovered here.

The Countryside Agency say that Historic Landscape Characterisation, a process not yet devised in 1964 when the AONB was designated, would now be one of the main processes used to help define a boundary. Perhaps this would rule out some of the strange anomalies which seem to have arisen in this instance.

Calder Vale, meanwhile, is a fine example of a village conceived and constructed around an industrial heart, in this case a mill for weaving cotton. Built by two Quakers, Jonathan and Richard Jackson in 1835, in addition to the mill there is a terraced row of 19 workers' cottages (rather unimaginatively named Long Row) and a manager's residence. The mill continues to thrive today, though it is no longer powered by the River Calder, and the geographical restrictions of the setting have meant that there has been no expansion of the village to speak of, so it remains a classic example of a small industrial community.

At one time there were many small industrial enterprises within the heart of the AONB, not just around its perimeter. There were bobbin mills, fulling mills, silk and cotton mills, small quarries and limestone kilns. These occupations are often reflected in the names of roads long after the jobs and even the premises have disappeared completely.

Opposite: *Traditional mill workers' cottages at Calder Vale.*

TEN BUILDINGS OF CHARACTER

The Court House, Bolton by Bowland
Old Well Hall, Downham
Long Row, Calder Vale
Browsholme Hall
Hornby Castle
Newton Hall
Twiston Manor
Town Head, Pendleton
Roughlee Old Hall
Halton Green

The impressive gateway to Browsholme Hall. Note the stag on the wall to the left of the arch.

Opposite: *The Court House at Bolton by Bowland dates from 1704. The court was held upstairs on the right with the cells below.*

Above: *Newton Hall.*
Below: *Hornby Castle above the River Wenning.*

5. Rough Uplands and Fringe Farmland

The uplands are characterised by a sense of vastness which is out of all proportion considering the relatively small area when compared with other European wildernesses. Skies seem to stretch forever and the rolling moors have a distinct sense of isolation, despite the proximity of major conurbations.

The treeless, often saturated, moorland is covered with coarse grasses, stands of rushes, blanket bog and, where the ground is better drained, a thick carpet of heather which provides huge swathes of purple when it is in flower. In this grand vista the lines drawn are generally smooth and flowing with only occasional gritstone outcrops breaking the pattern. At slightly lower altitudes there are sharply

Rough grazing on Longridge Fell.

Opposite: *Farms dot the landscape around the upland core.*

cut stream beds, known locally as cloughs, and scattered woodlands which provide blocks of shadow within the picture, here and there a slash of stone wall or a glimpse of narrow winding road reminds us of the human influence.

Much of the rough moorland lies above the fell wall, the upper limit of enclosure, with stone walls almost exclusively predominating though isolated stretches of wire fence sometimes provide a boundary where a previous one has either never been in place or has disappeared completely. Farmers generally try to maintain existing stone walls, but few would claim to have the time to install one from scratch should a new field boundary be necessary. There are no farms higher than 300 metres, with precious few above 240 metres. Other than occasional grouse butts, and tracks fit for four-wheel drive vehicles leading up onto the grouse moors, visible signs of mankind's attempts to tame the moors are few.

The fell wall divides pasture from rough grazing.

Opposite: Rushes dominate the plateau above Roeburndale.

Wild and windswept but colourful too.

Closely linked with the characteristic peat deposits of the upland fells are the podzol soils of the fell sides. Such soils are typically those in which the naturally occurring minerals and organic matter have been leached out of the surface layer, washed downwards by persistent drainage over a long period of time.

A typical cross-section would reveal dark, sodden peat with few stones but many fine roots in the surface layer. Beneath this might lie a fine silt consisting of the finest particles which have been washed through the upper layer but which mix only slowly with the more stony layers of clay or sandy loam which come next.

In some places the iron oxides washed out of the surface layers begin to accumulate above the lower layers of loam and these cement together to form a thin band known variously as ferricrete, ironpan or hardpan. This thin gravel layer can cement itself so successfully that it becomes impervious to water and effectively provides a seal between the deeper layers of clay or sandy loam and the peaty layers above. This ironpan layer prevents the mixing of organically rich peat and the mineral-rich loam resulting in excessive acidity, making the land unsuitable for anything but rough grazing unless it is dug deeply enough to break up the ironpan, with the probable addition of fertilisers or lime to adjust the level of acidity.

At first glance the uplands can appear bleak and featureless, especially where they form a rolling plateau, and they are far from being a species-rich environment. In fact the decline in upland bird species and localised over-grazing by sheep are genuine causes for concern. Even blanket bog has been lost in places due to the digging of drainage ditches which results in the drying out of the normally saturated plant communities which comprise the blanket bog.

Nevertheless, there is more to this wild windswept habitat than first meets the eye and small changes in climate are also beginning to have a favourable effect on some species. For instance, in sharp contrast to the decline of the ring ouzel and concern over the fragile breeding record of some birds of prey, stonechat numbers have risen markedly during the last decade due to milder winters. The United Utilities Bowland Estate recorded only three pairs in the late nineties, but in 2005 that number was up to 46.

Opposite: Sweeping lines and huge skies characterise the upland landscape.

A swathe of heather decorates Birkett Fell and Kitcham Hill.

Post Office Cottage in Abbeystead village, part of the Duke of Westminster's estate.

The moors are covered predominantly with blanket bog, sphagnum mosses, coarse grasses and reeds, with occasional cotton grass and even cranberry in places. The less well-known cloudberry is found here too, along with bog rosemary and pale forget-me-not which are both nationally scarce, along with the wonderfully-named lesser twayblade.

Expanses of heather can be found especially where the moorland has been managed for the purpose of grouse shooting, these areas often having been burned to encourage new growth. Young heather tips are favoured by caterpillars as well as by grouse and the blanket bog of the northern fells in particular has one of only two remaining colonies of large heath butterfly.

A well-managed heather moorland is likely to support a variety of birds of prey including the merlin, peregrine falcon and the hen harrier – the symbol of the AONB. In addition, easily-identifiable species like the curlew (an estimated 2850 pairs in Bowland), wheatear and ring ouzel, often known as the moorland black-bird, can be found, especially in early summer. Surprisingly perhaps, the Bowland fells are also home to one of the largest breeding colonies in the UK of lesser black-backed gulls, containing some 10 per cent of the UK's population.

It is impossible to write about moorland without including reference to the Abbeystead Estate, one of several large estates within the AONB. Owned by the Duke of Westminster since 1980 as part of Grosvenor Estates, Abbeystead is synonymous with grouse shooting in many people's eyes, not least the North West Hunt Saboteurs who have given the estate plenty to think about in recent years.

Abbeystead holds the world record of 2929 grouse shot in one day in 1915 but nowadays the numbers shot would probably average 350 brace (700 birds) in a day. Estate Manager Rod Banks has represented landowners and farmers on the AONB Joint Advisory Committee for several years and is well placed to understand the complexities, contradictions and conundrums which beset the many issues over which he must preside. He has to manage increased access to previously restricted moorland, balance shooting with conservation, oversee a twenty-year woodland action plan, manage a water catchment area, and help to maintain the viability of twenty tenant farms.

The management of grouse moorland means facing up to the realities of predation. While the uninformed image of raptors taking grouse chicks has a tiny element of truth in it, there is greater danger from foxes, whose numbers vastly outweigh the few birds of prey in the area. Past epidemics of parasitic gut worm have also reduced the grouse population in recent years as have the outbreaks of heather beetle.

The heather is managed by the controlled burning of strips in spring, which produces a patchwork of heather stands which vary in age, height and structure. This provides the best possible chance of a breeding environment not just for red grouse but also for a wide variety of other upland flora and fauna. It is noticeable that areas of heather upland not managed for grouse shooting have been quick to decline in recent years.

TEN UPLAND BIRDS

Buzzard
Curlew
Dotterel
Hen harrier
Red grouse
Ring ouzel
Short-eared owl
Snipe
Stonechat
Whinchat

Distance: 9½ miles (challenging) with five shorter options
Duration: seven hours   Start / finish: car park at foot of Parlick (SD 601441)

◆ This is one of the most varied routes in the whole AONB with plenty of interest along the way, including the possibility of seeing gliders flying from their base off Fiddler's Lane and people parascending from the summit of Parlick. At the end of the description of the complete route there are details of two alternative sections which can be used in conjunction with it to create six possible variations in total.

◆ From the car park take the private road heading north-east signposted Wolfen Hall Estate. Shortly after a left and right S-bend a path crosses it at right-angles. The stile is there on your right but there is no indication of the path to your left unfortunately. Turn 90 degrees left onto this until you reach the ruins of Wildcock

House then turn eastwards on a footpath which will take you right through Wolfen Hall. (Ensure that you are heading north-east as you leave the Hall as there is another right of way along a track heading south-east from Wolfen Hall.) The path takes in a foot-bridge then the northern tip of Wolfen Hall Plantation on its way to Saddle End where you will turn northwards.

◆ As you leave Saddle End the path forks and you need to take the left hand fork which will shortly lead you northwards along a track up onto Saddle Fell. It is important to continue heading due north as the track divides in numerous places (in fact, it looks like Spaghetti Junction at one point!) and, if presented with a choice, always take the right hand option as long as it's heading north.

Wolfen Hall Estate.

The private road to Wolfen Hall at the start of the walk, with Saddle Fell in the distance.

Stile on the section between Bleasdale School and Lower Fair Snape.

◆ You will shortly come to a green-painted bird hide which has been erected by the tenants of Lower Fair Snape Farm and which is freely available to walkers who wish to take time out to view the lapwings, redshank and oystercatchers which breed here. Looking due north from the hide you can see the copse in which stands the site of the historic Bleasdale Circle (see text above). Continue for another mile and a half in a south-easterly direction past Blindhurst Farm back to your starting point.

◆ Now for the two alternative sections. The first leads from the car park straight up the slopes of Parlick then northwards to the 510 metre summit of Fair Snape. From here some deft compass work across open and often saturated moorland will lead you north-eastwards for nearly half a mile to meet the original route. The second alternative is a path which runs in a consistently NNW direction from just east of Blindhurst (near the end of the original route) through Higher Fair Snape Farm to Hazelhurst (through which you pass following the descent from Fiendsdale Head in the original walk description).

◆ A mile and a quarter north of Saddle End the track will veer left through 90 degrees then peter out. From this point head due north uphill for 300 yards and you will meet a path running east to west. In fact, if your compass skills are accurate you should meet this path at a point where there is a boundary stone. Turn left, westwards, onto this path and follow it for just under a mile when it will swing NNW to Fiensdale Head. Your route then switches south-westwards, diagonally crossing the slopes of Winny Bank as you aim for Hazelhurst Farm. Continue in the same direction below numerous small plantations until you reach Clough Heads Cottages and Brooks Barn. Turn south-east past Brooks with its packhorse bridge after which take the right fork past Bleasdale School.

One alternative is a direct ascent of Parlick.

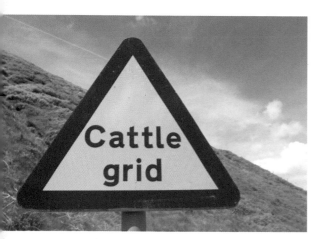

Cattle grids often mark the start of the upland core.

Typical moorland fringe farmland north of Chipping.

Opposite: *Isolated barn on high pasture between Wray and Roeburndale.*

THE MOORLAND FRINGE

The moorland fringe farmland described refers to the transitional belt of land which lies immediately below any land which has all the characteristics of the uplands described earlier. Traditionally, the demarcation between fell or rough pasture and the farmland below it has tended to be the last stone wall one reached as one climbed higher, often referred to as the fell wall. This would often be at a fairly consistent height above sea level meaning that, as the wall of one landowner contoured around the hill, it would be likely to meet the adjacent landowner's fell wall and continue to encircle the moorland or hillside. In some areas the fell wall might well be at a similar height to the highest altitude at which trees tend to grow. In this way, the upland area can sometimes be quite distinct.

In upland areas at generally lower altitudes, such as Exmoor perhaps, this demarcation is not as distinct as it might be in, say, the Lake District. While the fell wall principle works well in some parts of the Forest of Bowland it is not always the case; however, it is generally true that, where a road crosses the moorland, the distinctive upland character can be found above any cattle grid set into that road.

The critical factors determining the boundary between moorland and fringe farmland are soil and natural vegetation, drainage, and the extent to which farming practices have altered the balance. It is interesting to note that some farms at higher altitudes are situated on land that, from the map, one might expect to be moorland in character but which is actually green and productive pasture. The best example of this is around High Salter Farm, situated above Roeburndale at an altitude of 260 metres, at the northern end of the track known as the Hornby Road which traverses Salter Fell.

Fringe farmland in the AONB is generally typified by its enclosure, mostly but not exclusively, by stone walls constructed of gritstone or limestone, and by the predominance of stone-built farms and isolated barns. The land tends to be rolling farmland, generally falling away from the uplands and cut by deep cloughs with scattered pockets of broadleaved woodland which often accompany the cloughs themselves. In a few cases, stands of pines remain, often providing some shelter for exposed farms at higher altitudes.

The overall impression is one of a managed landscape yet one which is managed in the face of adversity, having to cope with harsh weather in winter and a wet climate for the remainder of the year, needing to brave persistent wind and unforgiving soils. Farmers here are a hardy breed.

The slopes of the undulating farmland between the fells and the valley bottoms are often cut by steep-sided and wooded cloughs, carved by substantial streams which flow steadily all year long. In the north and west of the AONB such streams are invariably also the locations of substantial clusters of broadleaved woodland, such as around Roeburndale and Artle Dale.

Some of the most attractive features of fringe farmland are these small pockets of trees, barely substantial enough to be called woodland in many instances, which are found on the often steep-sided banks of the many streams which pour off the moors. These clough woodlands break up the views of expansive moorland while also providing a useful variation in habitat in an otherwise windswept and largely shelterless environment.

Opposite: *Clough woodland near Oakenclough.*

They are, however, very much at risk simply because of their isolation from other woodlands and natural regeneration is by no means guaranteed. Sheep farmers are

95

Note the rapid transition from the exposed rock strata of Clougha to the flat pastures of Quernmore.

encouraged to fence in these clusters of trees to prevent further destruction of ground level plant growth.

Where young valleys drop quickly from the moors, the transition from upland through fringe farmland to valley pasture can be rapid. Stone walls are suddenly exchanged for hedgerows and wooded streams thread their now more leisurely way towards broader and shallower valleys where they join more established rivers. Roeburndale is such an example. Occasional stands of beech are sometimes located where limestone outcrops occur.

Lower down the slopes the stone walls are replaced by hedgerows and increasing signs of land management are visible. Farms are more frequent, small hamlets have developed and isolated inns occur outside the small villages which have usually grown around central features like a crossroads, river crossing or village green.

DIVERSIFICATION AND STEWARDSHIP

The trend towards diversification is having impact on a large scale in the Bowland area. Whole swathes of land formerly used as pasture, for instance, are subject to large-scale management practices involving substantial sums of money because agricultural funding in the EU is the largest single purse into which any member country can dip. When this fact is allied to EU directives on the conservation of wildlife, the packages of funding available are considerable and are tapped into by many of the organisations and agencies referred to in this book.

An estimated one third of the AONB's farms are in receipt of some of this funding for a wide variety of projects, making an overall examination of the situation impossible in the space available here. It is perhaps more useful for the reader to look at how one such project works.

Breeding waders on the rush-rich pastures of fringe farmland are of great importance, both nationally and locally, with an incredibly high proportion of the UK's lapwings favouring the area. Each spring over 6000 pairs of wading birds are attracted by Bowland's wetter fringe farmland, predominantly lapwing, redshank, curlew and snipe.

The RSPB's Wader Project is especially active in the AONB and participating in one of the Wader Safari walks is enlightening, not just from an ornithological point of view but also from a land management perspective. There are two key reasons why waders are so important: firstly, they are very territorial and will favour the same

Curlew.

Below left: *RSPB Wader Safari walk.*

Below right: *Expert knowledge is shared by the leaders of RSPB walks.*

fields year upon year. Secondly, they often grow to a ripe old age, given the chance, in comparison with many other birds. The RSPB's Tom Bridge tells a wonderful tale of one occasion, when he worked in Norfolk, of handling an oystercatcher whose ring markings proved that the bird was at least thirty-six years old.

To illustrate the changes that wader management regimes have brought to the landscape, it's helpful to examine one particular example. Lower Fair Snape Farm is a tenant farm a couple of miles north of Beacon Fell Country Park and part of the Bleasdale Estate, sitting snugly below Fair Snape Fell which is on the ridge stretching northwards from Parlick. When Robert Gardner moved to the farm as a boy in 1953, the fields were knee-high in rushes and the greatest need at that time was to try to drain fields. Rushes thrive on such land with its high water-table and with their incredible self-regenerative capacities: each rush stem produces in the order of 10,000 seeds and they have a very high colonisation rate compared with other plants.

Since the Gardners' decision to join the Countryside Stewardship scheme in 2000, things are very different. The ten-year plan to which they are committed actually involves 're-wetting' some of their land, rather than draining it, in order to encourage waders. This is done in part by creating 'scrapes' which fill with water to provide a mixture of standing water, much of it shallow enough for chicks, and areas of soft mud in which the oystercatchers, lapwings and redshanks can feed. These scrapes are of particular importance during April, May and June because they encourage breeding birds to stay in the locality.

Rush-management has become much more scientific in recent years. Gone are the old methods of spraying and the much more selective technique used now is called rush-wiping. Basically, the fields are mown in late July or August once the breeding season is over. (That may seem rather late but these birds will have a second or even third attempt at breeding if initially unsuccessful.)

The rushes are allowed to grow again and then they will be wiped using a machine set at a height which will treat the rushes but not the other grasses. The rushes are literally wiped, rather than sprayed, with a glyphosate treatment which keeps them in check. The net result at Lower Fair Snape is managed rush cover of between five and ten per cent but it is an expensive process, costing around £100 per hectare.

Rushes thrive in the wettest conditions.

Bird hide on Lower Fair Snape Farm.

TEN FRINGE FARMLAND BIRDS

Lapwing	Peregrine falcon
Oystercatcher	Pied wagtail
Kestrel	Redshank
Meadow pipit	Skylark
Merlin	Wheatear

Lapwing.

Oystercatcher.

In addition to these measures the Gardners have planted areas of new woodland and hedges, and have even constructed a bird hide close to one of the largest scrapes. It is on a public footpath through the farm so it is freely available to the public. In addition to the lapwings, oystercatchers, redshanks and the occasional snipe on view there are large numbers of brown hare also.

It should be explained here that the Countryside Stewardship scheme has been replaced by a new two-tier Environmental Stewardship scheme though projects originally launched through the Countryside Stewardship scheme, like the one in place at Lower Fair Snape, will see out their ten-year plan.

Money for stewardship projects comes direct from DEFRA but farmers may, and often do, add to this by seeking additional sources of funding for projects which are complementary to their stewardship, woodland grants for example. It should be understood by the reader that the impact of stewardship schemes on the farming landscape is quite distinct and farmers cease traditional sheep and cattle farming in order to join these schemes. The funding for such stewardship is based upon the income which has been 'lost' through giving up other methods of farming.

Fields full of cows and sheep are apparently replaced by 'empty' fields, and casual visitors to the area are often surprised by this. It is only through spending time in the AONB and learning more about the management of farmland that visitors will understand, and benefit from, the changes taking place.

99

Fringe Farmland Walk: Tarnbrook and Marshaw Wyre

Distance: 6½ miles (easy / moderate) Duration: four hours
Start / finish: roadside parking near Tower Lodge (1½ miles west of Trough of Bowland)

◆ The stretch of road near Tower Lodge is one of the most beautiful in the north of England. Shaded by stands of ancient woodland, it runs alongside Marshaw Wyre which, when joined by Tarnbrook Wyre, becomes the River Wyre which lends its name to this area: Over Wyresdale.

◆ Parking on the verge beside Marshaw Wyre, take the track (signposted Wyre Way to Tarnbrook) northwards from Tower Lodge, past the young plantation on your right to the gate at the western end of the newly replanted Tower Plantation. Continue north on the concessionary footpath signposted White Moor along the stone wall to a point where you meet a stile and a track running east to west. Pay heed to the warning sign about what to do if you find an unexploded shell from the days when the army used the area as a firing range.

◆ Having crossed the stile turn left (signposted Tarnbrook) and follow the wall until you reach a stile with the remnants of a sheepfold to your right. Cross the stile and head 45 degrees to your right for 30 yards to a gate. You are now back on a public footpath and should follow the wall downhill next to the strip of broadleaved woodland on your right. The path will take you

The bridleway from Tarnbrook to Gilberton.

The route through Abbeystead Estate is delightful in spring.

Ancient woodland by Marshaw Wyre.

Between Ouzel Thorn Farm and Top of Emmetts you will encounter one particular field which, according to the map, requires you to follow the field boundary. There is no longer any physical boundary in place but the line of it is still quite clear on the ground and you should follow this.

◆ The footpath emerges onto the road just east of Higher Emmetts Farm and continues immediately across the road. Continue westwards for three-quarters of a mile until you reach Strait Lane, having to pass through the garden of one of the estate cottages in order to do so. This seems strange but the route of the path is clearly marked and there's no need to worry about being intrusive.

◆ Turn left to follow the road downhill briefly, past the entrance to Abbeystead, until you reach a junction with a gated road off to your left (not signposted) immediately before Stoops Bridge, which is a splendid spot for a lunch break. There is a small car park here which could be used as an alternative starting point for this walk.

between the two barns (a nicely sheltered and very peaceful spot for a break) at the bottom of Spreight Clough and through Gilberton Farm, from which point it is designated as a bridleway. After crossing the bridge at Gilberton the unsurfaced track swings north-west leading into the delightful farming hamlet of Tarnbrook.

◆ Follow the road through the hamlet of Tarnbrook until you see a footpath sign on your left indicating a farm track which leads out of the hamlet, re-crossing the stream. The waymarked footpath then heads south-westwards across enclosed fields between Emmetts Wood and Ouzel Moss. (Be careful not to take the farm track also running south west from Ouzel Thorn as it ends abruptly by a barn on the hillside on your left.)

◆ Take the gated road and after 40 yards you'll find the Wyre Way footpath on the left which is signposted Marshaw. Continue to follow this eastwards through the estate, a section which is absolutely delightful in spring when the bluebells are out, along the course of Marshaw Wyre. Follow the infrequent marker posts, ignoring both a tempting crossing point and a footbridge, until you reach a footbridge on the left of which is a grotesquely-shaped tree overhanging the river.

◆ This is the correct route and about half a mile further on you will arrive at a ninety degree bend in the road which you rejoin, turning right, leading you back past Marshaw Farm to your parking place.

6. Steam Engines, Scarecrows and Hobbits

It is often assumed by town-dwellers that the things that bind small communities together are predominantly either the local pub or the village church. It is true that frequency of contact with one's neighbours plays an important role in a small community, but nothing binds people together like a huge joint effort, even though it may occur only once a year. For that reason, Chipping and Wray deserve close attention for their Steam Fair and Scarecrow Festival respectively.

If a sense of history is an important factor in creating a village community then Chipping has a 1000 year head start, having been mentioned in the Domesday Book.

Chipping Steam Fair.

Opposite: *Wray Scarecrow Festival.*

Chipping Steam Fair.

The 1925 traction engine 'Friend Richard'.

Chipping Steam Fair.

Add to that the village shop which has served local residents continually since 1668 and an Annual Steam Fair each year during the Bank Holiday weekend at the end of May, and you have a recipe for enduring community spirit. There is also the matter of Chipping's industrial heritage, despite its elegant rural character, for as many as seven mills once lined Chipping Brook, though only one survives today as home to the renowned chair manufacturing company, HJ Berry & Sons Ltd.

It is worthwhile digressing for a moment to take a look at this company as it is committed to a policy of ecologically sustainable development, as promoted in the AONB Management Plan. The company actually uses off-cuts and shavings to heat the factory, which emits no smoke and is more environmentally friendly because any carbon dioxide emissions are from what is known as the 'current carbon cycle' as opposed to those from fossil fuels. Over 95 per cent of its timber, mostly temperate hardwoods, comes from within the British Isles from managed woodlands and they guarantee to plant a tree for every dining set made.

Drystone walling demonstration.

The company works in close partnership with Lancashire Rural Futures and are members of the Woodland Trust, Woodland Heritage, and Lancashire Wildlife Trust as well as being actively involved in the creation of a number of ponds to further aid bio-diversity in the Bowland area.

Originally conceived as a one-off affair, the first Chipping Steam Fair was held in 1998 to raise funds for a new Village Hall. A staggering 10,000 visitors and 450 exhibitors attended that first show, with numbers over the next two years increasing further. Although the Foot and Mouth outbreak necessitated the cancellation of the 2001 event, hard work by the local residents who made up the organising body re-established the Steam Fair on the village calendar in 2002 only to be knocked back once more in 2003, this time by heavy rain which rendered the show ground unusable.

The following two years saw the Steam Fair grow from strength to strength, as well as benefiting from a new location just outside the village. The 2006 event saw a magnificent turn-out despite a very boggy car park: testimony to a labour of love on the part of all the organisers, especially Harry Slater and Mary Harrison. New additions to the event included a drystone walling demonstration and, without doubt the most popular display of all, several aircraft engines including a lovingly-rebuilt and gleaming Rolls Royce Merlin engine.

Inn at Whitewell
Hark to Bounty, Slaidburn
Dog and Partridge, Chipping
Coach and Horses, Bolton by Bowland
The Spread Eagle, Sawley
Parkers Arms, Newton in Bowland
Copy Nook Hotel, Bolton by Bowland
The Lower Buck Inn, Waddington
Gibbon Bridge Hotel, nr Chipping
Assheton Arms, Downham

The legendary Hark to Bounty inn at Slaidburn. The old Halmote Court used to settle local disputes in the courtroom upstairs.

Left: *Parkers Arms at Newton.*

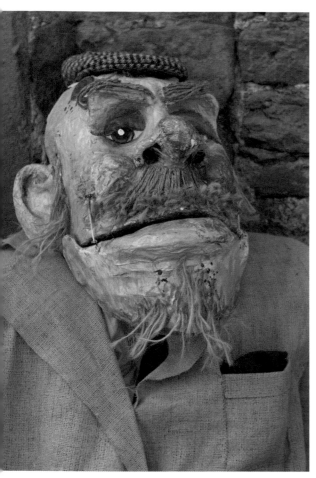

Wray Scarecrow Festival.

WRAY SCARECROW FESTIVAL

Wray is located in the north-western corner of the AONB just east of Hornby, which lies on the A683 from Lancaster. The majority of its 460 residents are extremely active in making their traditional village a better place to live and there are village activities throughout the year. There is even a fortnightly 'cinema' in the Village Hall, complete with big screen and surround sound.

But it is its annual Scarecrow Festival, started in the early nineties by local residents David and Frances Hartnup (after witnessing a similar spectacle at the village of Campan in the Pyrenees while on holiday), for which the village has achieved fame. It starts on the Saturday a full week before the first Bank Holiday Monday in May and money raised by the festival helps to fund a variety of local causes and development projects.

The ten-day festival, reaching its climax on the Bank Holiday, sees local arts and crafts on show, a variety of weird and wonderful events (like maggot racing!) and the sale of scarecrow memorabilia. The Bank Holiday weekend is obviously the busiest time with hundreds of families coming from far and wide to see the spectacle, to be part of the myth and magic, and to make the most of the rides, stalls and activities on offer. Though queues can build on the winding approach roads, parking is plentiful in a field at one end of the village.

Many Wray households display one or more scarecrows outside their homes: some in the gardens, some on the roofs and even some climbing walls and drainpipes. Each year there is a theme for those modelling new scarecrows. Past themes have included: the Olympics, James Bond, Hammer House of Horror, and Icons of the Century in 1999.

There are always the traditional 'Aunt Sally' and 'Worzel' styles in evidence too, along with some quite imaginative and eye-catching oddities: the rear end of a cat sticking out of a 'broken' door, above which a sign reads 'Who moved the cat flap?' Or a sparsely dressed skeleton in a garden chair below a sign reading 'Waiting for the perfect man'! Classic figures to be represented often include the vicar, the local bobby, Postman Pat, Humpty Dumpty, Gandalf and many more.

Even the most casual visitor cannot fail to appreciate the hard work which has gone into creating individual scarecrows, but the overriding impression is that of a

The Scarecrow Festival is a great opportunity to poke fun at famous people.

A patriotic note to some displays can be expected during a World Cup year.

More characters from Wray Scarecrow Festival.

sense of community. The Festival takes a lot of planning and success is only achieved through the co-ordinated efforts of a large proportion of Wray's resident population.

HURST GREEN, STONYHURST AND JRR TOLKIEN

With the recent film success of Tolkien's *Lord of the Rings* it seems appropriate to dwell on the origins of Middle Earth's topography, reputed to have direct links with this area. South-African-born JRR Tolkien, who died in 1973, often visited Stonyhurst College, on the south-western edge of the AONB, and spent many hours writing parts of his famous work in a classroom on the upper gallery of the college.

His son John was studying for the priesthood at the Jesuit seminary of St Mary's Hall which was part of Stonyhurst and later to become its preparatory school. Tolkien, an Oxford professor at the time, visited him regularly. His name appears

Stonyhurst College.

111

in the guest book many times between 1942 and 1947 and he is known to have delivered lectures here occasionally during that period as well. (His son Michael later taught Classics at Stonyhurst too, during the late 1960s and early 1970s.)

When he was not writing, Tolkien, who loved the countryside, spent many happy hours walking in the area. It was on these walks, it has been suggested, that he got his inspiration for some of the places described in his stories.

Stonyhurst College itself dates back to the thirteenth century and was extended considerably in later years. An Elizabethan house, initially built by Richard Shireburn in 1590, took another 250 years to be completed. During that time, in 1648, Cromwell spent the night here prior to the Battle of Preston.

Following the death of the last of the Shireburn family, the ownership of Stonyhurst passed to a Dorset family who never occupied it and allowed it to fall into a state of disrepair and it eventually found its way into the hands of a Jesuit English College based in Liège who were anxious to escape the consequences of the French Revolution. Stonyhurst thus became a Catholic boys' boarding school and has flourished as such ever since.

The guest house in the college grounds where Tolkien stayed, New Lodge, is suggested as the partial source for Tom Bombadil's house in the first chapter. Frodo is described as running to the eastern window and looking out onto a kitchen garden in which bean poles stood out prominently against the backdrop of a grey-topped hill, the beans' red flowers in stark contrast to their wet green foliage.

During 1947 Tolkien drew a colour sketch depicting New Lodge's garden complete with runner beans in full flower. Admittedly, this drawing was done looking towards the back of the house and not eastwards towards Pendle Hill, but the runner beans connection is surely a strong one and the grey-topped hill to the east could only be Pendle.

Another local feature which Tolkien knew well was the ferry across the Ribble, a couple of miles east of Stonyhurst and Hurst Green. It was still running in his day, though it ceased to operate in the fifties, and it may well have served as the source for Buckleberry Ferry which Frodo used when he left the Shire on his quest.

On the far side of the river lies Hacking Hall, the supposed inspiration for Brandy Hall, which would make the Hodder the Brandywine River. Tolkien's Great East Road, some would have us believe, was the much more humble B6243 which today crosses the Hodder over Lower Hodder Bridge. The triple-arched packhorse bridge standing beside it was built by Richard Shireburn in 1562 as a replacement for the wooden bridge which had existed here for at least two hundred years previously. Known as Cromwell's Bridge, it would have been Brandywine Bridge in the story.

Few of the names in *Lord of the Rings* provide obvious associations with Stonyhurst and the countryside around it. As well as the Shireburn family connection, in the village of Hurst Green nearby there is a Shire Lane. The River Loudwater, flowing from Rivendell, could only be the River Loud, a short river which flows into the Hodder at Loud Mythom just 3½ miles north-west of Stonyhurst. Loud Mythom, incidentally, means Loud Mouth and it is spelled Mytham on the map rather than Mythom, which is the spelling still used by those living there.

Barn at Loud Mythom.

Apart from the above, there are many place-names in the story which could possibly have links with the area, but it is by no means cut and dried. Tolkien writes of the

White Downs and it is not uncommon in the Bowland area for dales to have a 'white' side and a 'dark' or 'black' side, according to whether they face south or north. (It has also been suggested that 'black' moorland is comprised of greater than 50 per cent heather cover and that 'white' moorland has less then 25 per cent heather.) The White Side of Tarnbrook Fell is just one example. Then there is the Witch Realm of Angmar, the notion of which could easily have come from Pendle, and The Lonely Mountain which could have been Pendle Hill.

It is also noticeable that a number of place-names could have been anagrams or corrupted anagrams: many places in this area begin with the word 'Deer-' and Tolkien invented a number of places beginning with 'Ered'. Likewise, some places in the north-west (particularly the Lake District) have the suffix '–thwaite' meaning a clearing and Tolkien used the suffix '-waith' which may have been a corruption of

Cottage at Hurst Green.

Tolkien's imaginary River Lhun was surely derived from the River Lune, photographed here at Loyn Bridge.

this. There are also places in the story ending in '-dell' or '-dale' which obviously have northern connotations.

It would also be so easy to say that Buckland really stands for Deer Forest and so it could represent one of the old hunting forests. Finally, the very shape of the coast-line of Eriador, Rohan and Gondor is not unlike the shape of the Lake District. You can see how easily links *could* be made with the north-west and with this locality in particular, but that doesn't mean that they should.

Tolkien was determined that *Lord of the Rings* should be a very precise creation, right down to his spelling of certain words. He was furious and frustrated with his publishers who at times insisted on 'correcting' his spelling, for example 'elven' which the publishers amended to 'elfin'. Given this attention to detail on his part, it seems unlikely that Tolkien would be so obvious as to simply take a local place and use its name in the story.

Yet all writers at all levels *do* use their experience and observations in their work and it is quite reasonable that this should show through from time to time. In actual fact Tolkien went out of his way to de-regionalise his topography, with Downs, Wold, and Dale all featuring along with other place-names typical of different parts of the UK.

Personally, I believe that Tolkien's topography confuses people who try to draw associations with different localities for one very good reason: he has introduced a variety of scale into the equation. For instance, we have a small number of clear-cut localised examples such as the Loudwater probably being the River Loud, which is only a few miles long. But by the same token, Tolkien includes in his topography a long chain of mountains running all the way from Angmar to Isengard which, it could be argued, are a representation of the Pennines.

I think it is true to say that the topography of northern England and the north-west in particular certainly did have an influence upon him. Whether you wish to believe that Hurst Green is Hobbiton and so on is up to you. If you want to follow this up in more detail then there is a 5-mile circular walk from Hurst Green following some of these purported connections. It starts and finishes at the Shireburn Arms.

The Shireburn Arms at Hurst Green.

7. Woodlands, Rivers and Reservoirs

The Forest of Bowland's woodlands fall roughly into three groups: isolated stands of trees which, though few in number, provide important habitats in an otherwise empty landscape; continuous ribbons of broadleaved woodland along both younger and more established river valleys and, finally, managed plantations with by far the largest being Gisburn Forest.

Smaller pockets of broadleaved woodland are often grouped around the sharply-defined cloughs dropping off the hillsides, especially in the north and west of the AONB. Historically, these have often been the favourite haunt of the ring ouzel, but

Larch woodland floor.

Gisburn Forest from the road over Bowland Knotts.

Opposite: *The Lune is one of four main rivers draining the AONB.*

Conifer plantations can be dark and eerie places.

TEN WOODLAND BIRDS

Chiffchaff	Long-eared owl
Crossbill	Nuthatch
Goldcrest	Pied flycatcher
Green woodpecker	Siskin
Chaffinch	Tree creeper

Chaffinch.

this rather shy species of thrush has declined dramatically in numbers of late, both locally and nationally, with its numbers being halved over the last two decades. For instance, known ring ouzel territories on United Utilities' Bowland Estate have dropped from over 30 to barely a dozen during this period.

These pockets of clough woodland, together with the continuous valley woodlands, typically contain a wide variety of plants at ground level in sharp contrast to the conifer plantations which support no ground cover whatsoever, being so devoid of light that on a dull day it can be really quite dark beneath their high canopy. Many of these blocks of coniferous forest are of similar age, and it is only in more recent years that the wisdom of mixed species planting has been applied.

Classic woodland sites include the remnants of ancient woodland along Marshaw Wyre and the northern valleys of the Artle, Roeburn and Hindburn. These last three have very limited access both by car and on foot and have consequently retained much of their inherent character, containing oak, birch, ash, alder and rowan trees. Ground flora often includes bilberry, bluebell and wood anemone, along with the distinctive swathes of wild garlic.

The lower in altitude in these young river valleys, the richer the variety of ground flora encountered and the greater the variety of wildlife, from small mammals to badgers and foxes. The knock-on effect is seen in the birds encountered, too, with the tree pipit, redstart and pied flycatcher being more common, not to mention the occasional sparrow hawk, for whom this is rich hunting territory.

But it is important never to lose sight of the fact that all habitats in the AONB are fragile and that the survival of specific species can never be taken for granted. A case in point perhaps is Gisburn Forest with its large area of established woodland, now containing a mix of coniferous and broadleaved species, and a good variety of habitat around its fringes. Despite this promising habitat, nightjars have failed to breed here for several years.

Of course, there may be darker reasons for this. The eggs of some species, despite being protected by the Wildlife and Countryside Act (1981), are a popular target for thieves whose punishment when caught rarely fits the crime.

Hogweed.

Pink purslane is found in damp woodland but is rare across much of England.

119

Woodland Walk: Beacon Fell

Distance: 3 miles (easy) Duration: One and a half hours
Start / finish: Beacon Fell Visitor Centre car park

◆ This choice, starting from the Visitor Centre at Beacon Fell Country Park, is ideal for walking the dog (on a lead, of course), taking younger children on a nature ramble, or just as a pleasant stroll on a summer's evening after tea.

◆ It is worthwhile collecting from the Visitor Centre a free leaflet on the Country Park, which has a large scale map on the reverse side. This shows the different blocks of woodland and main features along with three trails. The Fellside Trail is a circular route devised for off-road cyclists and it may also be used by horse-riders by prior arrangement with the Countryside Ranger. There is a short Sculpture Trail linking the three sculptures in the Park and, lastly, there is the Woodland Trail which is another circular route taking in some of the most typical blocks of woodland and the summit of Beacon Fell itself. A brief diversion via the tarn is easily achieved.

◆ This walk utilises sections of both the Fellside and Woodland Trails described briefly above. Leaving the Visitor Centre car park to your right, follow the short stretch of cobbled path which soon gives way to compacted stone and then forest floor as you enter the magnificent tunnel of Larch Avenue, following the Woodland Trail. Even on the brightest of days, children will find this place dark and eerie with its starkly-silhouetted tree trunks rising parallel into the tree canopy above, among which birds flit and sing but are hard to spot.

◆ Larch Avenue takes a turn eastwards below Shield Wood (so named for its shape) before the trees open out at a crossroads. Turn right onto the Fellside Trail and follow it a short distance to the tarn. It is worth lingering here, strolling around it to sample

its different aspects, before carrying on to meet the road leading to Quarry Car Park, the upper of two car parks with the other being Quarry Wood Car Park. (This road is sometimes closed to cars during the day by a barrier and is always closed at 5pm.) Turn left onto the road and follow it into the car park from which a short set of steps leads up to rejoin the Woodland Trail, heading westwards now, towards the 266 metre high summit.

◆ After reaching the Country Park's highest point continue to follow the track gently downhill for 50 yards until you reach a crossroads just after the sculpture of the bat which is hard to spot, hidden in the trees to your left. At this path-junction turn right onto the Fellside Trail again and follow this westwards through Queens Grove, past the pond in Dewpond Wood, until you reach the one-way road which encircles the fell.

Left: *Sculpture at Beacon Fell Country Park to commemorate its 25th anniversary.*

Below: *Beacon Fell Tarn.*

Trig point at the summit of Beacon Fell.

DISABLED VISITORS

◆ Lancashire County Council have funded two all-terrain electric buggies which are available at the Visitor Centre, free of charge, to the disabled once they have had some initial training, which takes half an hour at the most. Specifically designed to cover rough ground, mud, grass and forest tracks, these buggies can follow three suggested marked routes within the Country Park but must be booked in advance by telephoning the Visitor Centre.

◆ Cross the road into Spade Meadow via the stile and turn left, following the line of woodland until you reach the gate leading back into the Visitor Centre. The open vista of the plain as far as Morecambe Bay is all the more exhilarating after the confines of the forest.

◆ Much of the above walk can be followed using one of these buggies with two exceptions: the steps linking Quarry Car Park with the track to the summit, and the final section through Spade Meadow. The tarn is so attractive that, in the case of the first exception, it is worth visiting it and then retracing one's route to pick up the track to the summit, which able-bodied visitors join further along after climbing the steps from Quarry Car Park.

◆ A wide variety of habitats are encompassed in this walk from the Tarn, which is home to no fewer than 11 different dragonflies and damselflies, to the meadows in which the late evening sun will pick out the almost translucent ears of a brown hare or, if you are very lucky, a roe deer. The woods themselves are alive with birdsong from goldcrests, tree pipits and a variety of finches, while great spotted woodpeckers may also be heard drilling away from time to time and seasonal visitors such as the brightly-coloured crossbill may reward a patient and observant visitor in spring.

◆ In the case of the second exception, while it may not be possible to walk through Spade Meadow, the road can be followed the short distance back to the Visitor Centre and some of the same views can then be had by crossing the road outside the Visitor Centre and covering the 20 yards or so of track leading to the gate into Spade Meadow.

Inset: *Dragonflies and damselflies are plentiful around Beacon Fell Tarn.*
Top right: *Route marker for Tramper electric buggies for the disabled.*

TRICKLES AND TORRENTS

Infant streams across the AONB spring from the sodden peaty hillsides at frequent intervals with many carving distinct paths down the hillsides, joining forces in the steep-sided young valleys which are characteristic of the fringe farmland. But the peaty trickle of hillside streams can soon evolve into a tumbling torrent, as the residents of Wray in 1967 would vouch. It was on 8 August of that year that the normally placid Roeburn found a destructive power so great that it washed away two bridges and three houses entirely, with a further 10 houses being damaged beyond repair. Where that row of houses once stood there is now a memorial garden.

These established but relatively narrow and fast-flowing streams have carved their way through the soft surface bedrock, winding their often tree-lined way towards the broad meandering major rivers which drain the area. The Hodder is the best-loved of these, from its shallow rock-strewn beginnings above Cross of Greet Bridge throughout its transformation into a broad, meandering thread linking Dunsop Bridge and Whitewell. Here it passes though a wide flat-bottomed valley with pastures denoting its extensive flood plain, surrounded closely on three sides by the heather-topped fells which feed it.

Though the Hodder drains the south of the AONB and the bulk of the uplands lie to its north, it is still this part of the region which typifies the AONB for many people. In the far north west of the AONB, the Lune which runs through it, though a grander river in terms of scale, does not have the same mountain character as the Hodder, and the same can be said of the Ribble which passes through the south-east corner of the AONB. While both Lune and Ribble have waymarked footpaths for considerable stretches along their banks, they tend to attract fewer day-visitors than the Hodder and their focus tends to be different too. You won't see the same proliferation of walking poles and map cases, but you will see more families and dog-walkers.

The last of the four rivers draining the area is the Wyre, the upper reaches of which consist of Marshaw Wyre and Tarnbrook Wyre (see the Fringe Farmland Walk). Marshaw Wyre is traversed on the way up to the Trough of Bowland from the west, its gentle meanders cutting deep into its peaty banks to reveal the root systems of the pines which shade its progress. Sadly, early in 2006, a number of the larger trees were felled, but it remains one of the most visually stimulating stretches of water course in the whole of the North West.

The Inn at Whitewell.

Opposite: *The infant Hodder at Cross of Greet Bridge.*

Distance: **8** miles (easy) Duration: five hours
Start / finish: Dunsop Bridge car park

◆ Turn left on exiting the car park and follow the road a short distance until the left hand bend. At this point a right of way follows the road to Thorneyholme Hall which leads off on the right hand side of the road. On approaching the Hall take the path to the right, past the Hall itself and follow the east bank of the Hodder 2 miles until reaching Burholme Bridge. (At one point along this restful stretch of river it sweeps through a huge meander, level with Burholme Farm, but the path does not follow the riverbank: instead you must continue straight on through the farm.)

◆ On reaching Burholme Bridge either take the concessionary path along the river or continue along the road to the Inn at Whitewell and St Michael's church adjacent to it, then turn left up the hill with Porter Wood on your left. When you reach a small stand of trees on the left with disused quarries visible opposite, look for the footpath on your left heading for the southern tip of Raven Scar Plantation where the stone wall meets the woodland boundary.

◆ Continue to follow this path in a generally easterly direction cutting through Browsholme Heights Wood and Crimpton Farm eventually to emerge onto the road north from Cow Ark. Turn left onto this road and just after Marl Hill House take the footpath on your left in a north-westerly direction aiming to the right of Kitcham Hill.

◆ As you walk this section up onto the fringes of Birkett Fell, which is thick with purple heather in season, you will cross the route of a Roman road though now there is little to indicate its former presence. When you are due east of Kitcham Hill the path swings northwards, just after negotiating a gully.

124

Entrance to Thorneyholme Hall at Dunsop Bridge.

◆ As the path comes level with the bulge of Birkett Wood to your right it arrives at the corner of an enclosure where there is a ladder stile, beyond which it veers NNE to Higher Birkett Farm, now running close by Birkett Brook. At Higher Birkett the path forks and you can take either route the short distance downhill to the interestingly-named Giddy Bridge.

◆ There are two equally attractive possibilities here. You can take the path north-east via the footbridge over the Hodder then swing northwards to come out onto the Newton to Dunsop Bridge road just east of Boarsden. Immediately after Boarsden take the footpath on your left, following the river's north bank back to the bridge crossing the Hodder to Thorneyholme Hall and back into Dunsop Bridge.

◆ Alternatively, you can head north-west from Giddy Bridge along the track (which has permitted footpath status only) past Knowlmere Manor and through Mossthwaite to Thorneyholme Hall and Dunsop Bridge. This last option saves about half a mile and will make only a marginal difference to the duration of your walk.

Churchyard at the parish church of St Michael at Whitewell.

Burholme Farm and meadows beside the Hodder.

The walk circles Kitcham Hill, seen here from Burholme Bridge.

Shelduck.

Goosander.

WATER CATCHMENT

The reservoirs of the area are easily divided according to scale. Stocks Reservoir is the only one of any real size, in terms of either surface area or volume. During the late nineteenth century, the Bowland and Pendle water catchment area began to be used for providing water for towns in Lancashire.

However it was not until the 1920s that construction began on the dam which ultimately created Stocks Reservoir. When it was completed, the farming community of Dalehead and Stocks in Bowland were casualties of the deliberate flooding of the valley and all except the church and its attendant graveyard was lost. The church was reconstructed above the reservoir and the graves relocated there too.

Much more recently, on 12 March, 2003, Stocks Reservoir was the location for perhaps the rarest of bird sightings in the AONB: a white-tailed eagle was spotted by the RSPB's Peter Wilson and Rod Taylor. The largest of the sea eagles, its blue wing-tags later helped to identify it as one of 10 which had been tagged as fledglings the previous year in north-west Scotland.

A very depleted Stocks Reservoir.

Scene on the path linking Stocks Reservoir and Gisburn Forest.

Lower Ogden Reservoir.

The RSPB's Peter Wilson spotted a rare white-tailed eagle over Stocks Reservoir.

Stocks is not as accessible as one might hope, with not one inch of its shoreline bearing a public right of way, though a permitted footpath does follow a short stretch of the western shore. Both its western and eastern aspects can be followed to some degree by public footpaths which run to within several hundred yards of its shore in places but public access in this area has had its emphasis placed heavily on the adjacent Gisburn Forest.

Of all the reservoirs within the AONB, those on the slopes of Pendle Hill are undoubtedly the easiest to access on foot and are extremely popular with walkers using the village car park in Barley. Nature lovers also favour the attractive wooded shores of the reservoir at Abbeystead. Sadly, the reservoir and its pumping station at Abbeystead are remembered by many as the scene of a disastrous explosion which killed 16 people in May, 1984. The fatalities were among a group of around 40 visitors attending a presentation in a valve house set into the hillside when a build-up of methane gas exploded.

Distance: 5½ miles (moderate) Duration: three and a half hours
Start / finish: Barley car park

◆ Starting from across the road from the car park, follow the bridleway past Barley Green Farmhouse and the Nelson Waterworks building then continue along the United Utilities access road, which is surfaced as far as Lower Ogden Reservoir. Follow this westwards along the north shore.

◆ At the reservoir's western end the bridleway is joined by the Pendle Way, which this route follows until after the steep descent

of Big End, and which is signed regularly along its route. At Upper Ogden Reservoir's dam the bridleway makes a sharp turn northwards but stay on the Pendle Way, now classified as a footpath, and continue heading westwards as far as several old sheepfolds whereupon the path swings northwards over the open ground of White Slacks as it climbs up onto Barley Moor. At the top of the rather ill-defined Boar Clough, the path swings north-east before joining a more-established path which leads northwards up the final slopes of Big End and its 557 metre summit.

◆ Continue northwards briefly before taking a diagonal route SSE which descends to Pendle House. Just before reaching this point the path forks; take the left fork for a short distance then turn left onto the bridleway past Pendle Side, emerging onto Barley Lane.

◆ Turn right onto the road and almost immediately is a footpath off to the left which is followed through Windy Harbour Farm and past Higher Laithe Barn to the wonderfully-named Salt Pie House with its views over Upper Black Moss Reservoir. From this point follow the path south to Foot House Gate and then there is a choice of heading along either the west or east sides of Lower Black Moss Reservoir back to Barley.

Top left: *Barley Green Farmhouse.*

Left: *Nelson Waterworks at Barley Green.*

Opposite, main: *Upper Ogden Reservoir.*

Opposite, inset: *Pendle Way footpath marker.*

128

Upper Ogden Reservoir

North West Water
a United Utilities company

This land is owned by North West Water for
water catchment and is a resource for the community

8. Bewitching Villages of Pendle Hill

The gruesome tale of the Pendle Witches involves curses, clay images, and bones stolen from fresh graves in the churchyard at Newchurch. It is enshrined in both English folklore and documented history and was immortalised in Robert Neill's novel *Mist Over Pendle*.

The tale begins with two families in the early seventeenth century, headed by elderly women who went by the names Demdike (real name Southern) and Chattox, whose real name was Anne Whittle.

The granddaughter of Demdike, who was called Alizon Device (modernised to read Davies in some accounts), spent much of her time begging and on 18 March, 1612 she accosted a pedlar who refused her repeated attempts to persuade him to give her some of his wares. Annoyed, she cursed him and, in an instant, a black dog is supposed to have appeared from nowhere; she instructed the dog to make the pedlar lame and he immediately became paralysed on one side.

Alizon Device was brought before Justice Roger Nowell at Read Hall and confessed to her witchcraft. She explained how Demdike had taught her to make use of a spirit to carry out her curses, in this case the spirit being that of a dog. As her tale unfolded, it became clear that her grandmother, Demdike, had also been involved in a sequence of events which had culminated in the death of the daughter of local resident Richard Baldwin. Alizon Device also revealed the witchcraft activities of Chattox, specifically making use of a clay image which she maliciously destroyed leading to the death of the innkeeper's son at nearby Higham.

Armed with the evidence of Alizon Device, Roger Nowell had Demdike, Chattox and Chattox's daughter Ann Redfearn brought before him (at Ashlar House near Fence rather than at his own residence, Read Hall) and, together with the

Opposite: *An imaginative likeness of a local witch outside Witches Galore at Newchurch in Pendle.*

The ancient route through the Trough of Bowland.

self-confessed witch Alizon Device, he committed all of them to stand trial for witchcraft in Lancaster. Their route to Lancaster would have taken them through the Trough of Bowland.

Further investigation revealed the complicity of Alizon's brother James, who admitted his part in another death through practising witchcraft, and their mother Elizabeth. Standing apart from these poor families, all of whom had long since been deemed by local people to be strange to say the least, was the clever and manipulating Alice Nutter who had been a powerful and influential person of good standing in the community up until this point.

However, there was enough evidence against her for Roger Nowell to commit her for trial too, also charged with witchcraft. Finally, on 17 August, 1612, all were convicted and sentenced to be hanged, with the exception of old Demdike who had died in prison while awaiting trial. The hangings took place in Lancaster three days later in front of huge crowds of onlookers.

Sadly, few of the buildings in the story of the Pendle Witches remain today. Chattox had lived in Higham whilst Demdike, together with her daughter Elizabeth Device and her grandchildren, at a dilapidated property, much less grand than the name suggests, known as Malkin Tower the exact location of which is uncertain.

Just outside the village of Blacko is a property called Malkin Tower Farm which was converted into luxury holiday cottages in 2002. It seems unlikely that the farm itself, which is too substantial a property, was Demdike's home but the remains of a cottage behind the farm could well be the Malkin Tower of the story. These remains predate other suggested locations on the same farm's land. An alternative location for Malkin Tower has been suggested as being in Malkin Field on Sadler's Farm close to Newchurch.

However, Alice Nutter's house was Roughlee Old Hall which does still exist. The present building is inscribed 'This house was builded by MN in the year of our Lord 1536', the MN referred to being Miles Nutter, whose son Richard was Alice Nutter's husband. Ashlar House, built in 1594, where Roger Nowell first questioned Demdike, Chattox and her daughter Ann Redfearn, also remains.

Roughlee Old Hall was the home of the 'witch' Alice Nutter.

Much of the action in this tale of witchcraft, the trial of which was exceptionally-well documented, took place just south and east of that part of Pendle which is within the AONB boundary but it is impossible to visit anywhere in Pendle which does not lean heavily on the story for visitor interest.

Perhaps it says something about our collective psyche that most of us find the tale of the Pendle Witches so fascinating, to the extent that it is attested at every corner in this part of the world and tourist literature covers it in minute detail, but George Fox barely receives a mention.

Few people will recognise the name but he was the founding father of a completely new Christian denomination: the Society of Friends, usually known as the Quakers. George Fox's birth followed closely on the deaths of the Pendle Witches in 1624, and he was a pious man who expressed great concern about the state of the Christian religion in England at that time. One day in 1652 he was moved to ascend the summit of Pendle Hill where he had a vision of a different kind of Church, and from that moment on he worked to create what became the Quaker movement.

St Mary's church at Newchurch in Pendle.

Nutter family gravestone from the seventeenth century.

NEWCHURCH IN PENDLE

The tiny former weaving and farming community of Newchurch has the best-known church in the area, St Mary's, with a church tower on which there is still the 'Eye of God' to ward off evil. Its graveyard (from which Chattox was accused of stealing bones) contains a grave marked with a skull and crossbones and a gravestone which is inscribed with the names of several of the Nutter family who died in the mid-seventeenth century, though not Alice of course. As for the skull and crossbones, it should be remembered that graves of those who died from the plague, which was prevalent in that century, often depicted a skull and crossbones.

Perhaps Newchurch's most famous claim to fame is a modern addition to the Pendle Witches' story: the Witches Galore shop. Its stark white facade acquires a more ominous tone with the addition of three full-size likenesses of witches outside the shop. Inside, it has a veritable treasure trove of witchcraft-related items.

Witches Galore attracts visitors from all over the world.

Designed to attract customers rather than scare them away.

BARLEY

The history of Barley dates back to 1324 when it was recorded as Barelegh. It has been suggested that the name equates to 'bare lea', meaning an unproductive meadow. It stands in the narrow valley between Stang Moor Top and Barley Hill in the lee of Big End, which is the summit of the scarp that forms the eastern side of Pendle Hill.

Barley has buildings dating back to the 1600s and was a farming community originally, with cattle being the mainstay of the village economy. With the coming of cottage industry in the eighteenth century, many of the cottages in and around Barley acquired handlooms, as did so many others around the cotton mill towns north of Manchester, until it ultimately had its own cotton mills. The mill at Barley Green in particular was successful enough to warrant 200 looms at one point, but it was destroyed by floods during the late nineteenth century.

Today Barley is best known as the starting point for many different walks. It is also a popular picnic spot with a small green and seating beside the brook. The 45-mile circuit of the Pendle Way, signposted throughout its length, passes through here but there are many local walks.

United Utilities has produced a series of leaflets on walks from Barley which include Upper and Lower Black Moss Reservoirs and Aitken Wood to the north as well as Upper and Lower Ogden Reservoirs and Fell Wood to the west. The combined capacity of the two Ogden Reservoirs stands at over 200 million gallons, with the combined Black Moss Reservoirs holding half that figure. Both the reservoirs and their adjacent woodlands are popular choices with bird watchers and with those whose walking is preferred without any sort of gradient.

SABDEN

The village of Sabden lies in the bottom of the valley drained by Sabden Brook, on the eastern side of Nick o' Pendle. The oldest part of this sprawling settlement, Heyhouses, is on its eastern periphery and there are a number of very old farmhouses remaining in the countryside around it. The oldest of these is believed to date back to the 1400s.

However, in the centre of the village is the Stubbins Vale Caravan Park and various light industrial premises. Development has been allowed to take place over the years with little apparent thought for any remaining character. The ubiquitous connection with local witchcraft is here, though, in the form of the Pendle Witch public house.

But there is another tall tale told hereabouts concerning Jeppe Knave Grave. Marked on the 1:25,000 map, just over a mile west of Sabden, Jeppe Knave Grave is situated on Wiswell Moor. It is an officially registered archaeological site, being classified in English Heritage's records as a Bronze Age cairn, and consists of a 'circular grass-covered mound 16 metres in diameter with a stone filled depression in the centre measuring 5 metres x 3 metres. This feature appears to be a mutilated cairn.' Different sources identify it variously as a round barrow and as a long barrow and, given its dimensions, one might be forgiven for preferring the word barrow to cairn.

The story is that during the eleventh or twelfth century, a local outlaw who repeatedly plundered the area around Pendleton, Wiswell and Sabden met his untimely end when unexpectedly caught by some of his victims. As no local parish could reasonably be expected to pay for his funeral, his body was dismembered and carried up onto the moor. Some accounts say that the exact spot chosen for his final resting place was at a point where the boundaries of the three villages met. One assumes that, as is usually the case, the Parish boundaries met at the summit, which would also have a cairn.

Unfortunately, the burial party mistook the Bronze Age cairn for the summit cairn, which is about a hundred feet higher. It would be an easy mistake to make in mist and rain, as the Bronze Age site is on a fairly flat shoulder just shy of the summit. Today the grave is marked with a carved stone to serve instead of a headstone, but this is undoubtedly a later piece of ornamentation.

Pendle Witch inn sign at Sabden.

DOWNHAM

This is undoubtedly one of the prettiest villages in the north-west of England. It has two notable residences in Old Well Hall and Downham Hall, ancestral home of the Assheton family since the mid-sixteenth century. There is a story that a large stone by the entrance to Downham Hall marks the resting place of two Roman

Above left: *Cottage garden in Downham.*

Above middle: *Beckside cottage in Downham.*

Above right: *Old Well Hall at Downham.*

Opposite: *Bridge over Downham Beck.*

soldiers but there is nothing to substantiate this, though it is known that there was Roman activity in the area.

The rebuilding of Downham Hall in 1835 in Georgian style disguises the fact that this building dates back to 1558. Similarly, the parish church of St Leonard's has been rebuilt, in this case as recently as 1910, around a bell tower which is over five hundred years old and which houses bells thought to have belonged originally to Whalley Abbey. The Assheton Arms, also at the top end of the village, was originally a farmhouse brewing beer for local workers which became the George and Dragon in 1872 and was renamed The Assheton Arms in the 1950s.

At the southern end of the village, on the wide main street just before the bridge over Downham Beck, lies Old Well Hall, which originated in the Tudor period. The banks of the shallow stream below the bridge, with its adjacent green, are popular places for a picnic in summer, with room enough for a number of parked cars without causing any congestion in the village itself.

Downham has caught the eye of location seekers from both TV and film industries, being featured in the 1961 Hayley Mills film *Whistle Down The Wind* and more recently having been used in the television series *Born and Bred.*

One striking reason Downham is popular with the visual media is that it is completely devoid of TV aerials and contemporary signs. Remove any modern vehicles and you have an instant period village. Even the original village stocks remain outside the pub and next to Stocks Tree Cottage. Incidentally, if you are planning to visit Downham from the direction of Clitheroe, it's well worth turning off the A59 to go through Worston and along the single track road around the back of Worsaw Hill as it's a delightful drive especially in spring with part of it being a designated Quiet Lane.

TWISTON

Twiston is a tiny hamlet to the north-east of Pendle Hill under the shadow of Big End and it rarely receives a mention in tourist literature on the area, or in any other literature for that matter. Yet it is a delightful place with no fewer than six listed buildings: Hill Foot Cottages, Hill Top, Red Syke Gate, Twiston Manor House, White Stones Farm and Lower Gate Farm. In fact, the only buildings in the village that aren't listed are Pendle Cottage and Manor Barn, itself the converted barn of the early-eighteenth century Manor House.

Twiston Mill.

Hill Top Farm at Twiston, one of numerous Listed Buildings in this small hamlet.

It's possible to drive right through Twiston without realising that you've done so. However, the penalty you pay for doing so is well worth it because you will have to drive up the hill towards Barley to turn round and, in so doing, you will be rewarded with one of the finest views over the Bowland Fells and Three Peaks.

PENDLETON

The village of Pendleton is actually a matter of yards outside the AONB boundary, but it would be churlish not to include it here, especially as it borrows its name from the brooding hill which towers above it. The stream tumbling down from Swardean Clough runs along the main street, occasionally spanned by stone footbridges, through the centre of this linear village which is old enough to feature in the Domesday Book of 1086. Its layout is typical of early farming villages with several farms scattered along the only street.

The most impressive property within the village lies on the south side of the street just before the school. Set back from the road, the Listed Building of Town Head is easily the largest and grandest property in the village, its understated facade a grand counterpoint to the huge coach house and stables set at right-angles to it. Close by is Fiddle Bridge, which once spanned the brook but now rests as a memorial to times past on a small green next to one of the farms. An even older artefact, a Bronze Age axe, now resides in the Museum at Clitheroe Castle having been

Fiddle Bridge at Pendleton is now purely ornamental.

unearthed during the building of a bungalow behind the Old Barn opposite the pub. This find in the late 1960s is from one of very few Bronze Age sites in the area.

Pendleton Hall lies just north of the village and was for nine generations the home of the de Hoghton family who now occupy Hoghton Tower, between Preston and Blackburn. (It was at Hoghton Tower that King James I famously knighted a loin of beef giving rise to the contemporary spelling of 'sirloin'.) To the south-west of Pendleton, the long, narrow fields running west to east clearly indicate the age of the village, with larger enclosures which would once have been common grazing land climbing the fell-side to the east of the village.

Today Pendleton enjoys its rural charm but also suffers from that same legacy. Its tiny village school closed twenty-five years ago, its only class reduced to just eight pupils, which was an even greater shame as it was one of the first National Schools in the country, opened in 1837.

The village school at Pendleton closed twenty-five years ago because of lack of pupils.

The Old Post Office at Pendleton.

The Old Post Office retains its postbox but has long since closed. Following its demise the village Post Office was run for thirteen years from the last remaining pub in the village, the Swan With Two Necks dating back to the 1770s, but even that facility has now gone.

The pub remains and, with it, one last anecdote to stir a smile. Pendleton doesn't have any tales of witches with which to beguile the visitor, but it does claim the most unusual auctioneer's story of a regular at the Swan with Two Necks who once sold his wife to the highest bidder!